Rewiring The Anxious Brain

Conquer Worry and Anxiety, Reduce Stress, Stop Overthinking and Calm Your Mind with Proven Strategies

Ian Tuhovsky

POSITIVE COACHING LLC

Contents

1

Introduction

Any productivity expert worth their salt will tell you that good or bad days are determined by the actions and inactions you took the night before. For the overthinker,
the night before kicks off with thoughts. As soon as your head hits the pillow, your mind
starts a movie reel of all the 'productive' things you could be doing instead of sleeping,
of all the mistakes you made during the day—and sometimes, throughout your life—and
of how nothing you do ever works. You think of the task you must submit in seven days
that you haven't started. Your partner has been acting weird lately. They are irritable and
absent-minded, and as you think about this project, you worry about your relationship
too.

Maybe they don't find you attractive anymore.

Maybe they are seeing someone else.

Or maybe, they want to end things and don't know how to say it.

This was exactly how it happened with your first relationship. You know the signs
all too well: First, they become irritable and distant. Then, they hit you with the "it's not
you, it's me." and suddenly, you are single again. The thought of registering on dating
apps, going on blind dates, and experiencing numerous talking stages is draining. You
reach out to touch their warm body, and they shimmy away from your touch instead of
snuggling into it.

See! says your brain. Something is wrong! They're pulling away.

So now, you think of the multiple reasons why they're pulling away. Was it because
you added a bit of weight? No, it's not that. Maybe it's because you haven't been as present
as you used to be. But it's not your fault—since you got this new job, things have been
hectic for you. Maybe they feel neglected and turned to someone else for comfort. Now
that you think about it, you saw them smiling into their phone a few days ago. They've
probably checked out of this relationship and into another one. Your heart squeezes at

the thought, and your eyes sting with unshed tears. It's already 1 a.m., you haven't slept a wink, and you have to be at work in seven hours. So now, you worry about not getting enough sleep and how much you're overthinking.

Somewhere amid this cyclone of disturbing thoughts, you eventually fall into troubled sleep. You dream about your supervisor reprimanding you for not delivering on the project and your partner leaving you for someone else. Just as they are about to introduce you to their new paramour, your alarm rings.

It's time to wake up.

You look at the time. It's 7 a.m. You just have one hour to get ready and get to work. You haven't even been up for a whole minute, and you are already worrying again.

Will I make it in time? Do I really need to eat breakfast? It'll slow me down. Today is Tuesday; the traffic is terrible on Tuesday. I might not make it in time. I think I'll skip showering. I showered last night. I'm pressed for time as it is. I cannot waste the little time I have showering. Maybe this is why my significant other is no longer attracted to me.

The thoughts keep buzzing in your head like judgmental bees, and they don't stop until you fall into troubled sleep again at the end of the day.

If this sounds familiar, then congratulations! You are an overthinker. You're probably a very logical person and might even have the phrases 'critical thinker' and 'able to work under pressure' somewhere in your CV. Both are your superpowers. You come up with creative solutions when every other person is in a creative rut. You are like Doctor Strange, analyzing a million possible permutations of a given problem and discovering different sets of solutions—with varying degrees of efficacy—for said problem. However, your superpower is your kryptonite. Like the guy that buys a Glock to kill a housefly, you often think up complex solutions to simple problems. Why? Because your mind has been wired to see threats, obstacles, and problems, even when there are none. This can be mentally exhausting. You find it hard to fall asleep because your brain "won't stop talking." And although you wished your thoughts would quieten down, deep down, you are grateful for them because they keep you safe.

In this book, we will take a holistic look at overthinking. We will look at:

- How the overthinking mind works

- The different flavors of overthinking

- The lies that encourage rumination and overthinking

- Why overthinking is different from self-reflection

- How overthinking is affecting your productivity, and the ability to form and maintain relationships and social connections

- Effective methods to curb overthinking.

2

A Deep Dive Into The Overthinking Mind

"*O*verthinking will not empower you over things that are beyond your control. So, let it be if it is meant to be, and cherish the moment . . .*"

Mahsati, A.

Erich Weisz (popularly known as Harry Houdini) was a man of many talents. During his lifetime, Houdini wore many hats. He was a magician, an actor, an astute businessman, a hobbyist pilot, and a history geek. However, the Hungarian-American went down in history as being the best escape artist the world had ever seen.

Houdini had a multiplicity of tricks under his sleeves, tricks that always awed his fans and critics alike. In one of his greatest feats, the Hungarian spent 91 minutes in a sealed underwater tank before escaping. Another version of this trick which he called the "Upside Down" (USD), involved him being locked upside down in a large water tank. After a few minutes, the anxious crowd cheered for joy; the master magician had escaped his watery prison! Houdini's tricks were as numerous as they were dangerous. The East Indian Needle Trick, for example, involved him swallowing a hundred needles and twenty yards of thread with a gulp of water. Then, like a mother bird feeding its young, he would regurgitate them fully threaded.

Houdini's skills became an urban legend. Everyone knew him and his taste for the adrenaline-inducing. The master magician claimed he could escape from any jail cell in the world in an hour if he were let in with his street clothes on. A lot of jail cells took him up on the offer. They would send him in and lock and fortify the doors. Unsurprisingly, Houdini was always out in a few minutes. He was the twentieth-century breaker of chains. Nothing, from straight jackets to manacles and jail cells, could hold him. Another very old jail down south decided to take Houdini up on his offer.

On the day of the event, numerous people gathered to watch the spectacle. Everyone wanted to get a peek at the urban fable that was Houdini. With a confident spring in his step and a proud angle to his shoulders, Houdini walked into the jail cell. The doors were closed with a loud clang, and the magician was left to his devices. Certain that he was alone, Houdini got to work. He shed his thick coat and retrieved a long, flexible, 10-inch piece of steel from his belt. Tools acquired, Houdini began to pick the lock.

Easy-peasy, lemon-squeezy, right?

Wrong!

Half an hour passed, and the lock still wouldn't budge. By now, Houdini's confidence had fizzled away like bubbles in a warm cup of Sprite. An hour later, he was sweating profusely, feverishly trying to get the lock to open. At the two-hour mark, the greatest showman of the 20th century gave up. He collapsed against the door, defeated, thinking of how he would face the adoring crowds and the sneering critics. With a gentle whine, the door swung open. Houdini couldn't pick the lock because the door had never been locked. It had always been open.

While many Houdini faithfuls have debated the veracity of this story, I believe it perfectly illustrates how the anxious and overthinking mind works. It is so used to encountering complex obstacles, problems, and threats, that it finds it hard to consider obvious solutions. Simply put, overthinking is the habit of thinking too long and too hard about something. With squinted eyes and a creased forehead, the overthinking mind analyzes every situation. A smile from someone is never just a smile. It is a sign that the other person is hiding a secret or silently gloating over something. The overthinker prides themself on being an expert in reading nuances, body language, and what is left unsaid. While some of these cues may be correct, they can also be wrong.

Let's go back to the example in the introduction for a moment. You think your partner has checked out of the relationship. You notice that your partner is irritable and distant and that they have been smiling more into their phone. You admit that you haven't been present since you got your new job, so you worry that you have "effectively driven them into the arms of another." One of the many unique things about the overthinking mind is that although it can contemplate multiple endpoints, it is sometimes quite unilateral in its thinking, often favoring the worst case scenario over other less damning ones. There are many reasons why your partner could be distant and irritable, reasons you may not be privy to since you haven't been as present as you used to be. Maybe they're having issues at work and haven't been able to bring it up with you because they see how happy and busy you have been with your new job. Upward mobility and life changes affect relationships, so maybe they're worried you might meet other people at your new job that you like better than them. Maybe you getting a new job has made them realize the need to pursue their dreams as intensely are you are pursuing yours. It doesn't always have to be all doom and gloom.

The second thing the overthinking mind does so well is personalizing. Everything is about them—or at least has to point back to them—in a negative way. If someone smiles at them, instead of smiling back, they start to worry:

Are they actually smiling at me? They can't possibly like me. I mean, I just blundered minutes ago. I spilled wine on XYZ's shirtfront. They probably think I'm a klutz and are only smiling at my awkwardness.

To solve this issue of personalization, you have to learn to contextualize issues. Life is not a houndstooth jacket, so things will never be black and white. There will always be shades of gray—and you have to pick those areas apart. Context is very important, especially when reading what is left unsaid. In the field of body language, for example, experts will often tell you that a cue can be interpreted in multiple different ways. So context is essential if you want to find out the right answer. Crossed arms may signal defensiveness or distrust. But it could also signal physical discomfort. The other person may be feeling cold or trying to hide a stain, or perhaps they realized their blouse is transparent under fluorescent light. It is not always about you.

Returning to the previous example with your partner—you notice they have been smiling more into their phone, which worries you. You touch their warm, clammy body at night, and they shimmy away. Right then and there, your fears are confirmed. The relationship is self-destructing. But that doesn't have to be the case. Maybe they're simply looking at memes and funny TikToks. Yes, them pulling away from your touch instead of leaning into it may indicate they are "unhappy." However, have you considered the option that the room was too hot and they were sweaty? Their body was clammy, and they had kicked away the sheets. Or maybe they were having a bad dream. There are a million and one reasons why they reacted the way they did, and usually, none of them have to do with you. But like Houdini, you always focus on the most difficult and emotionally draining option. Why? Because you have learned that expecting and preparing for the worst makes life bearable when bad things happen.

Nature, Nurture, and Narrative

When an overthinker catches themselves overthinking again, they beat themselves up and wonder, "Why am I like this?"

So why are overthinkers the way they are? Is it because of some genetic predisposition? A worrying gene inherited from somewhere in the family tree? Is it because of their environment? The fact that they work a stressful healthcare job, have defiant children, and manage an alcoholic partner? Or is it the story they tell themselves about their lives? The belief that everything they touch turns to dust, that everyone they love will always leave?

The answer? It depends.

Nature

Science has pinpointed a genuine biological predisposition to anxiety. The studies have also found comorbidity between anxiety and other mental disorders (like depression and Alzheimer's) and physical conditions (like irritable bowel syndrome, constipation, and palpitations). In a 2019 article, researchers argued that chromosome 9 is the stork bearing the gift of anxiety. However, some people with this same gene test negative for all the markers of anxiety. Proving that the biological doesn't have as strong a hold as we believe, the paper pegs the heritability component of anxiety at 26%. Put simply, if you have anxious ancestors in your family tree, there is a 26% chance you will be anxious too. Great odds, overall. However, this leaves the question: what determines the other 74%?

Another angle to the biological component is the brain chemistry debate. Whether or not it is linked to genetics or individual-specific defects, it has been observed that an imbalance of neurotransmitters can predict mood disorders like depression and anxiety. This is the fulcrum on which the monoamine hypothesis hinges. The monoamine hypothesis states that predisposition to mood disorders can be predicted by the depletion of three key monoamines/neurotransmitters: dopamine, serotonin, and norepinephrine.

Another chemical that can impact our anxiety is the stress hormone cortisol. When we are stressed, cortisol is released. In a feedback loop, the cortisol that is released to combat stress triggers more feelings of anxiety. However, we know that cortisol is never released without reason. Something has to trigger stress for it to be released. This brings us to the 74% from earlier and the nurture component of stress.

Nurture

The genetic component often leaves us feeling defective, believing we are marked from birth and destined for a lifetime of racing hearts and anxious thoughts. However, it is not completely true. Our environment plays an important role as well. Look at it this way. You may come from a long line of athletes with perfect health profiles ,and you may also express those genes in childhood. However, if you constantly binge on junk food, live a sedentary lifestyle, consume too much alcohol, and don't get enough sleep, you may develop health complications like obesity, diabetes, and hypertension.

For the nurture component of anxiety, the word "environment" is used to encompass:

The physical space we live in and its demands

Life circumstances

Lifestyle

The parenting we receive during our formative years

The social interactions we engage in

A person living in a war-torn country or a crime-ridden neighborhood is more likely to be anxious than someone living in a peaceful country or a quiet suburb. Danger, in any measure, facilitates hypervigilance, which in turn encourages anxiety. Another physical component that could affect your anxiety is the orderliness of your environment. Thus, it is no wonder why many young men across the globe took to Jordan B. Peterson's seemingly pedestrian advice of cleaning your room before you change the world. Your environment and your mood exert a complementary effect on each other. An untidy environment makes you feel disorganized on the inside and thus can lead you to be unhappy and depressed. Similarly, an unhappy and depressed person makes for an untidy environment. The small things like the color of your walls, how often you clean your living areas, smells, and lighting can have a huge effect on anxiety levels.

Life circumstances can also affect our anxiety levels. With the fluctuating hormones that come with pregnancy and menstruation, it becomes clear why women experience heightened anxiety during these periods. On a general scale, circumstances like abuse, trauma, poverty, and debt can trigger anxiety in a biologically anxious person. All things being equal, people working high-risk jobs (firefighters, policemen, etc.) and employment that demands a lot of their physical and emotional resources (scaffolders, construction workers, medical doctors) are more likely to be anxious than someone working as a receptionist or cashier. Parenting is also another predictor of anxiety. This is where epigenetics comes in. It is not enough to inherit a trait from your parents; sometimes, these traits need to be activated by certain environmental factors like bad diet, exposure to recreational drugs and unhealthy eating habits. This explains why in epigenetic studies using identical twins (specifically twins who were separated at birth), it showed that one twin would get cancer while the other didn't, although they have the same genetic composition.

The family is the first level of socialization, and within this unit, parents serve as models for their children. This modeling can be:

Positive: where a child (un)consciously emulates a parent's behavior e.g. viewing anxiety and hypervigilance as a form of protection and thus mimicking it.

Negative: where a child consciously rejects a parent's behavior template e.g. becoming more vigilant and anxious about relationships after witnessing how being too trusting affected a parent's life.

We can also develop certain habits that make us more anxious. Something as harmless as checking your social media pages upon waking up can set an anxious tone for the day. The same goes for things like not eating well (too much or too little, and good vs. bad nutrition), not sleeping enough or not drinking enough water daily.

The last element of environmental factors that affect our anxiety is the social interactions we engage in. This includes things like culture, interpersonal relationships, online interactions, etc. You may not be an anxious person, but if you are in an abusive relationship, things will change quickly. Abuse triggers the body's fear mechanism. To encounter the trigger (in this case, the abusive person), the brain has four options: fight, flight, freeze, or fawn. The abused person knows that no one reaction works every time with their abuser. For this reason, they are always analyzing, assessing, and reassessing which choice will elicit the least amount of pushback from the abuser at that point in time. This constant mental cartwheel is enough to make even the most disciplined mind overthink. Supporting this assertion, a 2000 research by Heim and colleagues shows that childhood sexual abuse primed and "sensitized" women for stress in adulthood. Further corroborating Heim's findings, psychiatrist Kenneth Kendler and his team of researchers discovered that major depression and generalized anxiety disorders were tied to traumatic life events like loss, divorce, abuse, accidents, and even racism. Based on this information, the mechanics of the manifestation of anxiety can be summarized thus:

Biological predisposition + stressful environment conditions = rumination/overthinking

However, there are people who do not succumb to overthinking and anxiety despite having the genetic predisposition and the necessary stressful events beforehand. This is where the third and final component comes in.

Narrative

In his harrowing holocaust memoir, Austrian psychologist and psychotherapist, Victor Frankl, writes:

"Everything can be taken from a man but one thing: the last of the human freedoms—to choose one's attitude in any given set of circumstances, to choose one's own way . . . every day, every hour, offered the opportunity to make a decision, a decision which determined whether you would or would not submit to those powers which threatened to rob you of your very self, your inner freedom; which determined whether or not you become the plaything to circumstance, renouncing freedom and dignity . . ."

Perspective is important but attitude is everything. This Frankl quote reminds me of a picture I once saw on social media years ago. The picture featured the top three winners of a race. The winner looked glum while the second runner-up looked as joyous as if he'd just broken an Olympic record. Looking at the boys' expressions, you'd have thought the position cards were wrongly assigned.

Attitude is key. Genetic predispositions and stressful situations aside, a person with a healthy, positive outlook on life can get through anything. Nature and nurture are important; however, narrative—the story we tell ourselves about our lives—is more important. The person that sees their trials as an obstacle they can overcome and the person that believes life is out to get them have different outlooks on life. This outlook is what makes the first person less likely to overthink, and the other more at risk for anxiety.

Retirement homes teach you a lot about life and the human mental process. Each segment of human society—poor, rich, male, female, educated and uneducated—is adequately represented there. While working in one, I learned valuable lessons from different residents. Ramona was one of those residents. She was a breath of fresh air. No matter how terribly your shift was going, entering Ramona's room was sure to uplift your spirits. She would ask how you were doing and genuinely listen to you recount your day. Each time her lunch was brought, her face became full of light and gratitude. Effusive. Before eating, she would thank God for the food and everyone taking care of her, pleading with this supernatural being to bless and repay her carers' kindness.

But here's the thing.

Ramona, a former nurse herself, was bedridden for life. And with her permanent confinement to the bed came complications like bed sores, reliance on others for personal care, and constipation. She also had mild dementia, but she was always a ray of positivity. Her outlook on life was infectious and made the emotional toll of working in a care setting bearable. She was always cheery and always mentioned how lucky she was to have people "looking after her and fussing over her." The small things like having her favorite meal delivered or watching her favorite shows gave her joy. Even when she spoke about her late husband, it was not with sadness but with a loving fondness and genuine gratitude for having done this life thing with him.

Being old and having to depend on others is not easy, especially if you have created a persona around your independence. Old age humbles you and brings you face to face with the things that truly matter. However, some people rebel against it. They become upset about their situation and transfer the aggression onto the people that love and care for them. "Don't grow old" was more or less an anthem with most people I cared for. They regretted not appreciating the privileges they had when they were young and actively despised the stage they were in. To borrow Frankl's words, most of them had traded in this last human freedom and submitted to the circumstances that threatened to erode their person.

While talking about factors that contribute to the creation of a narcissist, author and psychologist, Dr. Ramani Durvasula, talks about something she terms "a person's internal psychological resources." For her, it is that thing that predicts our individual reactions to certain stimuli (e.g., abuse.). For example, consider Sarah, Sally, and Sula. They grew up with an abusive mother who made their childhood an escape room of horrors. As an adult, Sarah is a terrible person and way more abusive than her mother. Sally, on the other hand, is a sweet and empathic soul with firm boundaries and healthy self-esteem. However, Sula, although kind, has no boundaries and is scared of her own shadow.

Looking at this, we glean that after exposure to a trigger, there is something that transforms our perception of that trigger. Dr. Durvasula calls this filter an internal psychological resource. I call it narrative, and it affects the modeling style we adopt after observing our parents'/caregivers' behavior. Sarah probably sold herself the idea that abusers are strong and only the strong survive. Thus, she strove to be strong. Conversely, Sally probably told herself the abuse she experienced was not her fault and that kindness doesn't mean weakness. Finally, Sula probably personalized the experience and went through life believing she deserved what happened to her.

Stories and narratives are important. On one hand, they can foster motivation. On the other hand, they can destroy wills. Most of us have talked agonized and talked ourselves out of formidable opportunities because of an ingrained, negative self-rhetoric:

Why are you applying for this job? You'll never be good enough to get in.

Sure, you got in, but we both know you will never fit in.

Nothing good ever happens to you. Stop dreaming. Keep your expectations low.

With this script in mind, you don't apply for jobs you are passionate about. Better to reject yourself first before they reject you. You don't step outside your comfort zone or try new things because nothing ever goes your way. You overthink favors, overanalyze people's feelings, and sweat the small stuff.

The Gender and Age Factor

While overthinking is an equal opportunity hitman, some groups are more likely to overthink than others. A study at the University of Michigan by Psychology professor Susan Nolen-Hoeksema shows that a whopping 73% of people between the ages of 25 and 35 overthink. Showing that overthinking tends to decrease as we age, the study also found that only 52% of people between the ages of 45 and 55 overthink. There are many reasons for this trend. First, your twenties are often a very demanding period of your life. Often tagged the defining decade, your twenties—all things being equal—and all the decisions you make within that period set the tone for how most of your life will be. Young people in this demographic often feel they should have it all—life, love, and career—figured out at this stage. Everyone is getting married and starting a family. Others are getting new jobs, moving to new countries, and getting advanced degrees. With all the changes they have to grapple with, it is not uncommon for young people to ruminate and worry about their choices.

Was starting a family now the right decision? With ChatGPT and how AI affects the workforce, will I really be able to re-integrate into a career when the kids are all in school five years from now?

Was focusing on my career a good option? With the fifteen-year fertility window in mind, maybe I should have focused more on starting a family instead of growing my career. Having a child in your mid to late thirties and applying for fertility treatments is a massive emotional and financial decision.

Was quitting med school and focusing on art a good decision? Yes, I am passionate about it, and I feel most alive when I paint, but passion doesn't really pay the bills. What happens when I am not able to get gigs? How will I be able to pay my rent and settle my student loans?

Like dementors, these questions keep swirling in your mind and drain you of energy. No matter which angle you analyze it from, you still cannot find the correct answer. Each side is rife with compelling advantages and worrying disadvantages. At the end of the day, you wind up where you started: thinking but never really taking a step. As we age, however, we come to the quiet understanding that nothing is guaranteed. That life will happen no matter how hard we fight and that the only thing we can really do is our best. Every other thing is determined by arbitrary laws of the universe. With age, you stop worrying about the failure that might come with some choices you make and learn to be confident in your ability to bounce back from those failures.

Nolen-Hoeksema's research also found that women typically overthink and ruminate more than men. The study also states that this was a factor in depression and interfered with "good problem-solving." Although stereotypes tell a small and skewed part of a very large and nuanced story, there is often some element of truth to them. Nolen-Hoeksema's research is one half of two research works that prove the common belief that women "worry a lot" is not just a misconception. Studies by California-based psychiatrist, Daniel Amen, and his team show that women's brains—especially the cerebral cortex, which governs impulse control and concentration, and the limbic area of the brain involved in mood and anxiety—are significantly more active than that of their male counterparts. Conversely, the parts of the brain that were more active in men were the ones that mediated visuals and image formation and coordination. Thus, explaining why men are more visual than women and more likely to excel at sports.

Amen emphasized the importance of assessing gender-based brain differences, as it illuminates gender-based risks for certain brain disorders. Their studies revealed that women had more blood flow in their prefrontal cortex, thus explaining why women generally have a more developed sense of empathy, intuition, self-control, collaboration, and appropriate concern. An elevated level of blood flow was also recorded in the limbic area, thus explaining why women are more likely to be anxious and suffer from insomnia, depression—which is a risk factor for Alzheimer's—and eating disorders. On the flip side, the parts of the male brain that received more blood flow were in the ventral, temporal, and occipital regions, and explained that men were more likely to have higher rates of ADHD, conduct-related problems, and incarceration.

Disclaimer: Some men will ruminate more than the average woman. On the other hand, some women battle ADHD. These studies do not ignore these nuances. However, while these people are important and should be recognized, it is essential to remember that exceptions do not make the rule.

Cogito Ergo Sum: Overthinking and Personality Types

In his quest to find an absolute, indubitable truth on which he could build a solid knowledge system, philosopher Rene Descartes created what is now known as the Cogito Argument.

Cogito, ergo sum.

I think, therefore, I am.

Descartes knew he could doubt a lot of things. His senses were not perfect and often presented him with false information. He could mistake a coat on a hanger for a man when the room was dark and might believe a straight pole was bent if it was placed in water. However, one universal truth remained amid this sea of doubt: In doubting things, Descartes was thinking.

Following this breadcrumb trail of thoughts, he chanced upon another concrete truth: anything that could think indeed existed. Thus, Descartes put together his argument:

Dubito, ergo, cogito. Cogito, ergo, sum.

I doubt, therefore, I think. I think, therefore, I am.

The method Descartes applied to arrive at his conclusion is called Methodic Doubt. The principal aim of this system is to find a single universal truth by doubting everything. Any knowledge that could not be doubted became an enduring truth. The only thing Descartes could be sure of at each point in time was that he was thinking, and if only existing things were capable of thought, then surely, he (Descartes) was existing.

Introverts and introverted personality types—like Descartes—are more likely to overthink. A common trend I see in discussions about extroversion and introversion is for people to assume that extroverts are outgoing and confident while introverts are shy and timid. Introversion has nothing to do with shyness and timidity. Yes, there are shy introverts. However, there are also timid extroverts. Introverts generally value solitude and need to be alone to recharge. A shy person, on the other hand, doesn't want to be alone but is afraid to interact with others.

Introversion and extroversion generally focus on how you obtain information and experience peak mental stimulation. The extrovert prefers to obtain information externally through discussions and social interaction. They are usually more energized and at the tip of their game in social settings. Staying indoors or introspecting for long drains them. They recharge their batters by rubbing minds with other people. The introvert, on the other hand, is a master at introspection. They gather information internally through thinking/introspection and reading. Unlike their extroverted counterparts, introverts are drained by social interactions. Thus, after intense socialization, they need to retreat away from people to recharge. Etymologically, the word "introvert" comes from two Latin phrases, "intro" (within) and "vertere" (to turn). Put together, the introvert is one who turns inward or concentrates on oneself.

For the introvert, thinking is a way of being. A way of remaining in touch with themselves and the world around them. This makes them very perceptive and intuitive. As they are always analyzing situations and putting themselves in other people's shoes, they are more empathic and the best listeners anyone could ever ask for. However, this thinking superpower that makes them very perceptive and skilled at reading a room, can quickly become negative if left unchecked. With overthinking, introspection—whether self or other-directed—can quickly become criticalness with overthinking.

Summary

- Overthinking is the habit of thinking too long and too hard about something.

- The overthinking mind is so used to encountering complex obstacles, problems, and threats, that it finds it hard to consider apparent solutions.

- Another thing the overthinking mind does well is personalizing. Everything is about them—or at least has to point back to them in a negative way.

- To solve this personalization issue, you must learn to contextualize issues. Everything is not and cannot be about you.

- Overthinking can be caused by any or all of three distinct factors: nature, nurture, and narrative.

- The nature argument advances that certain people have a biological predisposition to anxiety and peg the heritability component at 26%.

- Another angle to the biological component is the brain chemistry debate with the predisposition to mood disorders being predicted by the depletion of three key monoamines/neurotransmitters: dopamine, serotonin, and norepinephrine.

- Overthinking and anxiety can also be caused by the various stressors in our immediate and external physical and social environment (nurture).

- The narrative and the stories we spin about our life can also contribute to overthinking.

- A study at the University of Michigan by Psychology professor Susan Nolen-Hoeksema shows that a whopping 73% of people between the ages of 25 and 35 overthink.

- Showing that overthinking tends to decrease as we age, the study also found that only 52% of people between the ages of 45 and 55 overthink.

- Nolen-Hoeksema's research also found that women typically overthink and ruminate more than men.

- Studies by Daniel Amen and his California-based team show that the reason for the gender-based difference in overthinking is that the cerebral cortex and the limbic brain are more active in women than men.

- Introverts and introverted personality types are more likely to overthink.

- Introversion and extroversion generally focus on how you obtain information and experience peak mental stimulation.

- The extrovert prefers to obtain information externally through discussions and social interaction. The introvert, on the other hand, is a master at introspection. They gather information internally through thinking/introspection and reading.

3

The Seven Horsemen of the Apocalypse: The Primary Causes of Overthinking

"The sharpest minds often ruin their lives by overthinking the next step, while the dull win the race with eyes closed "

Bethany Brookbank

❈

To understand the "why" behind overthinking, overthinkers have a lesson or two to learn from cows, sheep, and goats

Yes, you read that right.

These animals have many things in common, and one of those commonalities is that they all belong to a class of animals called ruminants. Ruminants are herbivores with unique digestive systems. A digestive system with a four-chambered stomach. The four stomach chambers are the rumen, reticulum, omasum, and abomasum. When a ruminant grazes, the swallowed food goes into the rumen, the first chamber of the stomach. There, the food is partially digested and broken down into smaller chunks called cud. The cud is pushed into the second chamber (reticulum) and regurgitated into the mouth for thorough chewing. This process of chewing the cud/regurgitated food is called rumination.

Much like the rumination practiced by livestock, mental rumination is the process of chewing and continuously focusing on one or a specific set of thoughts. Ruminants ruminate (chew cud) because that is the only way to process and adequately digest their food. However, their human counterparts don't really ruminate (overthink) as a way to process their thoughts. There are seven reasons why we ruminate:

- A false sense of control

- Perfectionism and a false sense of safety

- A fear of positivity

- An unwillingness to lose focus of goals

- An intense need to please others

- Trauma or experiences

- Low self-esteem

1. A False Sense of Control

Overthinking has many rewards, one of which is a false sense of control. Over-thinkers have a huge fear of the unknown and a solid resistance to change. Like a juggler, the overthinker equates analyzing and juggling multiple thought networks to being able to control everything happening within and around them.

Meet Ruth, a product manager at a notable company. Ruth is phenomenal at her job. However, she burns out often and barely made a deadline. Ruth is a worrier by nature, and this not only drains her energy but also affects her creativity. At the start of work on Friday, Ruth's superior informs her that he'd like to discuss some pressing matters with her at the end of the day. Ruth replies with a calm, "Ok." However, her insides are fizzing and popping. If there is anything Ruth hates, it's "not knowing."

What exactly does the boss man want to talk about? Does he want to take me off the Anderson project? Is he annoyed that I submitted the last milestone five hours later than agreed? What's going on?

Ruth analyzed and agonized over the situation so much that she was barely productive throughout the workday. Letting go and not assuming the worst felt dangerous. She had gotten to where she was in her career through meticulous planning and analysis. It was her superpower. Without it, she felt powerless. Weirdly, she felt calmer when she thought of all the negative reasons for her boss's cryptic invitation. It helped her prepare for the worst. According to Natalie Dattilo, clinical health psychologist and Professor of psychiatry at Harvard Medical School, the brain sometimes believes it is productive by ruminating and worrying about a situation. The way it sees it, expending energy on something means it cares about it. Effort expenditure equals productivity. Hence, by agonizing over this, I am being productive.

At the end of work, a terrified but outwardly collected Ruth went to her supervisor's office. Wiping her sweaty palms on the seat of her pants, she knocked at the door. A gruff "Come in" sounded from the other side. Cautiously, Ruth pushed open the door. The man's face is buried in papers, but there was the unmistakable crinkle of a frown on his face. Ruth's heart was beating a tattoo into her chest.

He looked up at her. "Ah, Ruth. I have many bones to pick with you. The last milestone was late . . ."

Ruth was right. He was angry. She was going to be fired. She really needed this job. How would she pay the mortgage? Her partner only worked part-time, and the kids will start school next year. On and on, the thoughts swirled.

"Hello? Ruth? Are you even listening?"

Ruth was jolted out of her thoughts. "I'm sorry, I didn't catch the last part."

"It's my anniversary. I need you and the design team to come up with something. I want to surprise the missus."

"But what about the last milestone?"

"You were late. It's not a habit for you; it was just one time. Now, can we please focus on the anniversary thing?"

Ruth felt equal parts relieved and drained. Relieved because she still had her job but drained because she had spent the entire day worrying and preparing for the worst. If your overthinking, just like Ruth's, comes from a need for control, learn to delineate between what you can control and what you can't.

What You Can Control	What You Can't Control
Your reaction in face of any problem (e.g., you can choose to overthink a situation or not do so)	Other people's reactions (what your boss has to tell you or people's reaction to you)
The tasks you are currently working on (e.g., you can choose to give it your all or do a shoddy job)	People's perceptions of your efforts
The thoughts you choose to believe	The instant thoughts that pop into your head
Your perception of yourself	Other people's perception of you

Although her overthinking brain might say otherwise, Ruth had no control over what her supervisor wanted to tell her. The only thing within her control was her reaction to the situation. While it is okay to worry that something may be wrong, worry doesn't give us more control. If anything, it drains us of energy to act on the things within our control. Hence, Ruth should've focused on her daily tasks, completed them to the best of her abilities, and tied up any other loose ends.

2. Perfectionism and a False Sense of Safety

Do you often feel you have a grisly coach inside your head shouting terrible things at you and warning you to get your act together? Then your overthinking probably stems from a need to feel safe. While the first group of people overthinks as a method of control, this second group of people are perfectionists whose riotous thoughts are fueled by a need to always get it right the first time. Like the child that belts out the times table each time they want to do a simple sum, this overthinker believes they can avoid making mistakes by analyzing every imaginable situation and outcome, and preparing for all probable eventualities.

Joe is an exceptional writer who knows how to tell ordinary stories in unforgettable ways. The speeches he writes remain evergreen and evocative. The ad copies he crafts for the company website are the highlight of customers' user experience. Joe has a first-class degree in communications and writing, a cult blog following, and is currently writing his debut novel.

However, Joe has a big secret. Despite the thunderous applause he gets for his writing, he still doesn't feel good enough. Writing is not effortless for him.

If only his colleagues and fans knew how much energy he'd put in over the years to ensure his copies struck the right chord.

If only they knew how he'd agonized over every line before hitting "publish."

If only they knew how anxiously he waited for comments and validation from his readers.

If only they knew that this inadequacy he felt was why he still hadn't finished his book, despite being at it for the past seven years.

Each time he starts to write, Joe agonizes over every word. Is he overwriting or underwriting? Are his descriptions evocative enough, or is he writing purple prose? Is he using too many adverbs and cliches? Joe devotes three hours each day to his writing, but three-quarters of that time is spent thinking instead of writing.

Joe has a deadline to meet. He wants to submit his finished and edited manuscript to a known publishing house. He has one month left before the deadline. The publishing house is one of the most popular in the country, so the competition will be stiff. Joe knows he has to get his manuscript into the best possible state if he is to stand a chance.

But it turned out that as time went on, Joe wrote less and criticized more. Each time he opened the story, he found something that "needed more polishing." Joe never submitted that manuscript. As the deadline approached, he gave himself more and more reasons not to submit.

The work isn't good enough yet.

Everyone knows that submitting late ruins your chances of being accepted.

The world isn't ready yet for a story this radical.

People may cancel me for exploring the themes I do.

If your overthinking stems from perfectionism and a need to feel safe, you must rewire your thoughts about life and the issues it brings. Perfectionists see life as an endpoint, a milestone to be checked, and a key performance indicator to be achieved. So the thought of not checking those boxes terrifies them. This type of overthinker needs to understand that life is a process, not a product; a journey, not a destination. It is important to aim to achieve your goals. However, what is most important is the lessons you learn along the way. When you think of life as a product, you deny all the efforts you've put in and the skills you learned to get to where you are. Like Joe, you think you are just an imposter who got lucky. Let go and trust the process. You don't have to get things right all the time. Sometimes, by getting things "wrong," we find a new way of doing things.

3. A Fear of Positivity

We all know positivity is the opposite of negativity. However, this third group of people equates being positive with ignoring the existence of the negative. Healthy pessimism is important. After all, it is what kept our ancestors alive. By pulling from past experience, they could differentiate between friend and foe, predator and prey. However, pessimism becomes unhealthy when we see threats everywhere.

The overthinker who fears positivity probably has a laundry list of reasons why they should always be on their guard. Maybe an ex started cheating on them just when they began to settle into the relationship and buy into the whole "love" thing. Maybe a foster parent started abusing them just when they felt they had found a real home. Maybe they were betrayed by a friend they had always had implicit trust in. Whatever the reason, this overthinker has learned to fear the sunlight because, in their experience, there is always a chance of rain.

So they doubt everything and overthink even the tiniest of gestures. Every white or pink flag is poked and prodded till it becomes a red flag. If their partner sleeps off without texting, they assume their partner is cheating. A tiny disagreement with a friend becomes an indicator of a fracturing friendship. To solve this, you have to realize and understand that positivity is not ignoring the negative but rather overcoming it. Positivity is the acknowledgment that things are going well and the belief that you will be fine even if things go south. To learn to sit in and bask in the warmth of the present positive moment. Many overthinkers are living lives they dreamed about years ago. However, instead of enjoying their enriched realities, they are plagued by thoughts of everything that could go wrong. By rewiring your mindset and acknowledging you will find a way out even if things go wrong, it becomes easier to let go and enjoy all the things that are working out in your favor.

4. An Unwillingness to Lose Focus of Their Goals

Your alarm rings, and you snooze it for the sixth time this morning. You have to get up now or you'll be late for work. Despite getting eight hours of sleep, every muscle in your body is exhausted. You don't feel like getting up. You wish today was Saturday or Friday at the very least. But it's a bright and fine Tuesday morning. You still have three whole days of work before the weekend arrives. You try to get an extra minute or two of sleep, and that's when your brain goes off.

Do you want to lose this job?

You need to get up now if you want to get to work on time.

Remember the look HR gave you last week when you were late? Get up now!

Think of the rent. If you lose this job, that's it. Do you want to move back in with your cousin?

With these thoughts as background music, you push yourself out of bed and amble through your day. This is the basic template that your day follows. Each time you feel unmotivated or unwilling to do something, like an angry, underpaid coach, your mind "motivates" you into action by focusing on terrible things that could happen if you do not get your act right.

Lack of motivation to hit the gym is countered by vivid mental images of yourself battling obesity and heart disease.

An unwillingness to go out and meet romantic partners is met with caustic thoughts of dying alone surrounded by cats.

While this method can effectively make you put in the work, it is not sustainable. Honey always traps more flies than vinegar. Motivating yourself by thinking of the worst possible outcomes leads to burnout in the long run. Yes, you are afraid of the scenarios your brain paints. However, you are too fatigued—mentally and physically—to push yourself into action. To solve this, you have to:

- Focus on values, not outcomes

- Center on desirable positive outcomes instead of the negative ones

What are your values? Do you want to live a healthy life, spend time with your children, or pioneer a breakthrough in your field? Do you want to write books that will outlive you or create a company whose impact will forever be felt in your field? Do you want to help other people with your skills and talents? Will your job, workout routine, or current project contribute to this either directly or indirectly? If yes, then focus on that. Instead of focusing on how you'll flunk out of school (outcome) if you don't study, think of the inventions and breakthroughs you know you can make in your field in the future (value). Instead of thinking about how you might lose your job if you don't show up early (outcome), focus on how the money and flexibility you get from this job allow you to focus on your passion (value). The human mind tends to focus on the negative more than the positive. This is why negative thought processes effectively—albeit in the short term—shock us into action. However, like the person who chants the mantra "think of the money" as they undertake a project, obsessing and thinking about the negative reduces creativity and affects the quality of your work. So instead of focusing on losing your job (negative) to shock you into action in the morning, think of the fun you and your friends will have on your spring vacation (positive).

5. An Intense Need to Please Others

If your first thought when you walk into a room is, "How do I get them to like me?" you are probably a charismatic person. If your every waking thought after leaving the room is any variation of "Did they like me?" you're probably a people pleaser. Charismatic people aim to please within their means. The people pleaser overextends themselves in a bid to please and spends time worrying if the other person liked them. They ignore their needs in service of other people's needs and fight tooth and nail to always maintain the peace.

In the words of author and former president of the International Coaching Federation, Cheryl Richardson, "If you avoid conflict to keep the peace, you start a war within yourself..."

For Jennifer, the first cries of battle started with a splatter of pasta sauce on the hob. You see, Jennifer had a roommate named Chloe. Chloe was thoughtful, down-to-earth, and as friendly as a child hoping for an ice cream treat. After months of interviewing potential housemates, Jennifer felt a certain calm envelope her soul when she met Chloe. They had the same interests and worked in the same field. It was a match made in Craigslist heaven.

Ever the people pleaser, Jennifer prettied up Chloe's room before her move-in date. She vacuumed thrice, got new waste bins for the room and bathroom, and filled Chloe's ensuite with two months' supply of cleaning products and different shower gel brands. As Chloe wheeled her enormous bags in and took in the room, an anxious Jennifer waited for her reaction.

Does she like the touches I added?

She'd worn butterfly earrings to the interview, but maybe she thinks the butterfly lampshade is a bit too much.

What if she doesn't like the brand of shower gel I got? Or worse, what if she has sensitive skin?

Like an assembly line, Jennifer's brain kept pumping out thoughts as Chloe looked around the room. Chloe did the unexpected and pulled Jennifer into a quick hug. "I like the changes. Thank you!" For the first time that day, Jennifer's brain went quiet . . . for three whole seconds. Then the cacophony started again.

What if she was just being polite?

Had she hugged me to hide her disappointed reaction?

She probably thinks I'm creepy. The butterflies are too much.

It turned out that living with Chloe was everything Jennifer had dreamed of. There was only one problem: Chloe was a bit of a messy Bessy. Staring at the huge splatter of pasta sauce on the counter, Jennifer was unsure how to proceed. Chloe should know better. Clean up after yourself, especially after cooking, was one of Jennifer's five major house rules. Jennifer wanted to confront Chloe and calmly tell her to clean up, but she didn't want to be that kind of roommate. You know, the finicky type that people write about on Reddit's AITA threads. Besides, this was Chloe's second day at the apartment. Maybe she was just settling in.

And Jennifer was right. Chloe was just settling in.

Things got worse as the days went by. Plates were left unwashed for days. Stains from Chloe's "culinary experiments" polka-dotted the stovetop, the cabinets, and the counter. Each time Jennifer was gone seeing her parents, the garbage was never taken out, and the recyclables were always put in the wrong place. Jennifer was like Chloe's domestic guardian spirit, continuously cleaning up after her with a tight smile on her face and angry thoughts boiling in her chest. Each time she thought about confronting Chloe, her heartbeat quickened, and her palms sweated. Yes, she wanted Chloe to get her act together, but confrontations were uncomfortable. And she didn't want Chloe to feel uncomfortable.

The people pleaser's primary rule for interpersonal interaction is keeping the peace at all costs. People pleasers dislike and fear conflict and confrontation. For them, conflict is not an opportunity for growth, but rather a fight in the making and an indicator of a hemorrhaging friendship. They also have a scarcity mindset and believe that by being honest and upfront with their feelings, everyone will abandon them. Friendship to them is all about long-suffering self-sacrifice. They give their all in their relationships without expecting much from the other person.

Like the first group of overthinkers, the people-pleasing overthinker needs to understand the factors they can and cannot control and come to terms with them. In Jennifer's case, the only thing within her control was her response to Chloe's bad living habits (i.e., confronting/not confronting her). However, she was too afraid of Chloe's possible negative reaction, so she kept it all in. The second lesson is understanding that conflict can be sandpaper that refines your relationship. Nobody is perfect. Sometimes we need others to point out our shortcomings. It might be uncomfortable in the short term, but it makes for healthier relationship dynamics in the long run. Finally, understand that you are not responsible for people's reactions or opinions. The only responsibility you have on this earth is that of being a decent person. Sometimes by being honest and truthful, you will ruffle feathers and hurt people's sensibilities, and that's ok.

6. Trauma or Past Experiences

Etymologically, the word "trauma" comes from the Greek word traumatikos, meaning "wound," and what are wounds if not a calcified reminder of a painful incident? With trauma, the brain learns to associate a certain stimulus—that may be harmless on its own—with danger. To the child who was pursued by an angry goose, feathers and webbed feet are enough to set his heart racing. For a girl who has experienced abuse, a hug from a friend may be all it takes to return to the crime scene.

For eight-year-old Mary, heaven was a road trip. The sun glinting off the windshield of her father's Subaru. Elton John's mournful voice as he sang the tunes to Sacrifice. Her parents teasing each other and playfully bickering over the directions. The wind running loving fingers through her hair. And the games she and her brothers played to fill up the 4-hour drive. And no matter how many times her family took them, each road trip was a renewed experience in happiness.

This was before the crash.

Mary loved sitting by the window. It made her feel grown up. Besides, window seats offered the best views. It was the unspoken rule of road trips: Mary got one window seat, while her big brother got the other. Unfortunately, her younger brother wanted to feel grown up and drink in the views too. He did not understand why Mary who was just a year older got to sit by the window. So each road trip began with both of them fighting over the window seat. Thanks to her parents' interventions, Mary always won.

The day of the crash started like any normal day. Fighting over the window seat. Blues blaring from the speakers, and her parents bickering over which turn was the right one. Then her father took a wrong turn, and a truck smashed into the car, crushing Mary's precious window seat. It had all happened so fast. The realization that the truck was in the way; her mother's alarmed "look out!"; the squeal of brakes and the crunch of damaged metal. Mary closed her eyes and waited for death.

It didn't come.

What came was a spray of glass and the poke of mangled metal. She was safe. But the journey back home in the rental care was subdued. Neither Mary nor her younger brother wanted to sit by the window. The rejected middle seat became the cornerstone, the prime choice for the traumatized Mary. It's been seventeen years since that incident. Mary has rediscovered her love for window seats, but there's a gray cloud in her clear sky of healing: she is terrified of trucks. This fear of trucks makes her an anxious passenger and an incompetent driver. Each time she encounters a truck on the road, anxiety starts creeping in like termites through a rotten floorboard. She feels the sting of non-existent glass on her thighs, and in that moment, the twenty-five-year-old med student reverted to a scared eight-year-old.

With trauma and intrusive thoughts, it's a buy-one-get-one-free type of arrangement. When confronted with triggers, the brain tries to make sense of and come to terms with the trauma by pumping out a steady dose of disconcerting thoughts. As negative thoughts often beget more negative thoughts, these intrusive ones worsen the victim's rumination. This scenario is particularly evident with victims of abuse. They vacillate between replaying the events leading up to the abuse, thinking of what they should have done differently, and blaming themselves for letting it happen.

Also, trauma encourages hypervigilance. The traumatized brain disciplines and grooms itself to identify danger at all times. Like Uncle Max from The Lion King III, the traumatized person is always "scurrying, sniffing, and flinching" from perceived danger. They second guess everything because history has shown that danger is lurking at every corner. They fear strangers because strangers bring danger. However, they also fear friends because betrayal comes from those closest to you. Like a bird that flies without perching, they exhaust themselves by continuously sleuthing for danger even when there is none.

For the traumatized overthinker, the solution is therapy. Your incessant thoughts are the symptoms of a condition, not the condition itself. Getting to and resolving the root cause is the ticket to your freedom. If your trauma has been left unhealed for a long time, chances are your overthinking will be just as strong and might even make you too hard on yourself. While healing from your trauma, be patient with yourself. Engage your overthinking voice and counter all the opposing arguments it brings up. Remind yourself that your abuse and trauma are not your faults. Trauma-induced overthinking often manifests as an inability to trust one's instincts. So you must relearn to trust your own judgment. Remind yourself that the threat is gone and that now, you can settle into your skin comfortably and breathe fully.

7. Low Self-esteem

The perfectionist overthinker and the low self-esteem overthinker have two things in common:

They doubt their value (beauty, skills, talents, lovability, etc)

They attribute the good things that happen to them to luck and the bad to their unworthiness/mistakes/lack of skill etc.

For the low self-esteem overthinker, rumination is soothing and a way to gain reassurance. They are afraid of being judged and see every decision as a reflection of their self-worth. So they overthink every word they say, every picture they post, and every outfit they wear. Like Goldilocks, they always want to be on the "just right" end of the spectrum; no more, no less. Unfortunately, even when people think they are the next best thing after pineapple on pizza, they still doubt themselves. As the overthinking brain is adept at thinking up problems for each solution, for each compliment they get, they think up five reasons why they don't deserve it.

Derrick is the lead animator at an animation studio. His works have not only thrown the company into the limelight but have also opened up more work opportunities for Derrick. The entire art world is buzzing with news of the inconnu artist who took the art world by storm. Unfortunately, where people see talent, Derrick sees luck. Before posting any of his character ideations, Derrick scrutinizes it and sends it to multiple friends for feedback. As he waits for their reply, he tries to predict their reactions.

Why did it take Sarah three days to look at the samples? Maybe the work was terrible, and she didn't know how to say it.

Did Andrew really like the art, or was he just saying that to make me happy?

However, with each compliment his friends sent, his deflated self-esteem inflates. However, all it takes is one criticism or suggestion for improvement and all the helium hisses out. Derrick's low self-esteem also extended to his personal relationships. He always worried that his girlfriend would leave him. He could never really come to terms with the fact that she liked him for him. Yes, he was tall, but he wasn't fine and fit like her exes. As he was always worried she would leave him—or worse, cheat—Derrick never really enjoyed the relationship.

Like the perfectionist, the low self-esteem overthinker needs to unsubscribe from the product approach to life. You are more than your appearance, weight/height, and output. Your values and the content of your character are just as important. Decouple your self esteem from superficial qualities and focus on the substantial things that make you you. In our aesthetically driven world, appearance is highly valued. However, beauty fades, hairlines recede, and even the prettiest bodies—if they live long enough—wrinkle. The only thing that outlives all these are intrinsic qualities that endear people to you.

Also, learn to engage your brain each time it tries to make you feel inadequate. Counter its arguments and reemphasize your values. Losing or adding weight doesn't make you less valuable and worthy of good things. Remind it that you are not what happens to you. Failing at something doesn't mean you are a failure. You didn't have the tools to get it right the first few times. However, your comeback will be better. Another effective way of silencing this type of overthinking brain is bringing up a mental image of yourself at five years old and daring your brain to say all those negative things to the child you were. This is effective, as it triggers self-compassion and self-empathy and engenders objectivity. By centering our younger selves, we shed our bias and see our negative self-talk for what it truly is: a product of unrealistic expectations.

Ready to Dive Deeper? Unlock Your Exclusive Bonus Guides

Professional Resources + Ongoing Support, Tailored to Your Growth

Elevate your personal growth with access to **three short, professional online courses**, available in eBooks (PDF, EPUB, MOBI) and **audiobooks (MP3 files)**, plus an **exclusive email series** delivered to your inbox every few days.

Here's what you'll receive:

- **Enhance Your Communication Skills** – Build meaningful relationships and improve your social intelligence.

- **The Self-Discipline Blueprint** – Cultivate lasting focus and mental resilience to achieve your goals.

- **Mindfulness-Based Stress Management** – Practical techniques to reduce anxiety and maintain calm in any situation.

In addition to these guides, you'll receive a **series of 15-30 short, to-the-point emails** on your chosen topic, sent every 5-6 days. These emails are designed to respect your time while providing actionable insights, tips, and strategies to help you seamlessly apply what you learn to your daily life.

Rest assured, **you won't be spammed**. Alongside valuable guidance, you'll also receive **exclusive free and bargain offers** on books and audiobooks from the author, curated to support your journey.

By joining my mailing list, you'll unlock:

- **Free access** to all three guides (eBook and audiobook formats).

- A **personalized email series** to keep you inspired and motivated.

- **Exclusive tips, offers, and updates** on books, audiobooks, and courses designed for your growth.

Claim Your Free Guides and Email Course Now:

https://bit.ly/3freeguides

Think of it as having a **dedicated mentor in your inbox**, guiding you step-by-step toward a better version of yourself—**no fluff, just value.**

Summary

- Rumination is a process where certain herbivores chew regurgitated food (cud). In the psychological sense, rumination is chewing and continuously focusing on one or a specific set of thoughts.

- There are seven reasons why we ruminate: a false sense of control, perfectionism, fear of positivity, an unwillingness to lose motivation, a need to please, trauma, and low self-esteem.

- Overthinkers have a massive fear of the unknown and a solid resistance to change. Like a juggler, the overthinker equates analyzing and juggling multiple thought networks to being able to control everything happening within and around them.

- If your overthinking comes from a need for control, learn to delineate between what you can control and what you can't.

- For perfectionists, riotous thoughts are fueled by a need to always get it right the first time.

- If your overthinking stems from perfectionism and a need to feel safe, you must rewire your thoughts about life and the issues it brings. Perfectionists think of life as an endpoint, a milestone to be checked, and a KPI (key performance indicator) to be achieved.

- The perfectionist overthinker must understand that life is a process, not a product; a journey, not a destination. When you think of life as a product, you deny all the efforts you've put in and the skills you learned to get to where you are.

- The overthinker who fears positivity probably has a laundry list of reasons why they should always be on their guard. They equate being positive with ignoring the existence of the negative. So, they try as much as possible never to look at the bright side of things.

- To solve this, you have to realize and understand that positivity is not ignoring the negative but rather overcoming it. Positivity is the acknowledgment that things are going well and the belief that you would be fine even if things go south.

For the fourth group of people, rumination is a way to gain a firm grasp on their goals. They motivate themselves into action by thinking of the worst possible consequences of inaction. To solve this, you have to focus on values, not outcomes, and center on desirable positive outcomes instead of the negative ones.

- The people pleaser's primary rule for interpersonal interactions is keeping the peace at all costs. However, in the words of Cheryl Richardson, avoiding conflict to keep the peace is to start a war within oneself.

- The people-pleasing overthinker needs to delineate the factors they can and cannot control and come to terms with them. They also need to understand that conflict can be sandpaper that refines a relationship. Finally, they need to understand they are not responsible for other people's reactions or opinions.

- With trauma and intrusive thoughts, it is a buy-one-get-one-free type of arrangement. When confronted with triggers, the brain tries to make sense of and come to terms with the trauma by pumping out a steady dose of disconcerting thoughts. As negative thoughts often beget more negative thoughts, these intrusive thoughts worsen the victim's rumination.

- For the traumatized overthinker, the solution is therapy. Your incessant thoughts are the symptoms of a condition, not the condition itself. Getting to and resolving the root cause is the ticket to your freedom. While healing from your trauma, be patient with yourself. Remind yourself that your abuse and trauma are not your fault.

- For the low self-esteem overthinker, rumination is soothing and a way to gain reassurance. They are afraid of being judged and see every decision as a reflection of their self-worth. This type of overthinker needs to separate themselves from their metrics. You are more than your height, the numbers on the scale, and the amount in your bank account. Another effective way of silencing this type of overthinking brain is bringing up a mental image of yourself at five years old and daring your brain to say all those negative things to the child you were. This is effective as it triggers self-compassion and self-empathy and engenders objectivity.

4

Tag, You're It!: Signs That You're An Overthinker

"*This is probably the advantage of being stupid. Stupid people just do. We tend to overthink...*"

Sarah Strohmeyer

Every one of us has fallen into the trap of overthinking. It is natural and normal to overthink in the face of huge life changes like marriage, having kids, moving countries, or traumatizing events like the death of a loved one. However, overthinking now and then doesn't necessarily make you an overthinker. In this chapter, we will be looking at some of the markers of an overthinker. Overthinkers usually have a combination of three or more of these markers and experience them constantly and frequently.

Meta-Thought

This is the hallmark feature of the overthinking mind and simply refers to constantly thinking about your thoughts. So it is not enough that you are thinking what you are thinking, you are also thinking and worrying about what you are thinking. Meta-thought is like a secondary level of thought and it enables the overthinker to supervise their own thought process. Thinking for them often feels like a struggle between competing impulses. They try hard to steer their thoughts and understand every crevasse of their mind. In so doing, they question, doubt, analyze or judge their own thoughts.

After giving money to a homeless person, for example, an overthinker might think (in passing), "I hope he uses it for something good." However, because they are prone to meta-thought, another second layer of thought may question their motives for helping the homeless guy.

You feel happy and warm inside, the brain says. Giving a homeless guy money doesn't necessarily mean you are a good person.

Other people would have forgotten about the homeless guy minutes after the interaction but thanks to this penchant for meta thought, the overthinker spends hours trying to unpiece the thought process that motivated them into giving money to the homeless guy. Did they really want to help the man or were they unconsciously trying to advertise themselves as a good person?

Indecision

As we will see in the chapter on the different types of overthinking, indecision or analysis paralysis is a primary characteristic of the indecisive ruminator. They go back and forth over multiple options, talk it through with friends and agonize over the pros and cons of each option without making decisions. When all the options are swirling in their head, it feels like there is no right answer, like every solution is just another dead end. When they do decide, they spend the rest of the time second-guessing their choice and wondering "What if?" Confident people are not right always but are more willing to make imperfect choices. One mental tricks that keeps the indecisive overthinker undecided is the belief that their overthinking is actually a method of self-reflection. However, self-reflection leads to clear, decisive action while rumination leads to stagnation.

Lack of Concentration

Think of overthinking as trying to juggle multiple tasks at the same time. You are brushing your teeth, watching a Youtube video, texting friends, and editing a paper. While you might feel like you are being productive, you are actually not being efficient. All the tasks suffer as they are not getting the attention they require. It's kind of like running on a treadmill. There is so much motion but little to no progress. A 2003 study by Lyubomirsky and others found that overthinking, also known as rumination, damages your ability to focus. When we overthink, our brain gets cluttered and distracted. It assesses multiple possibilities and options without making a definite. So we stop making progress. If you find that you spend all your time thinking and less time doing, you are probably overthinking. This lack of concentration is also clearly seen in the social anxiety flavor of overthinking. Overthinking—as seen in social anxiety—is self-ish or self-focused. The socially anxious person is so wrapped up in their thoughts and their desire not to make a mistake that they cannot focus on the person in front of them.

Consistent Anxiety

In an episode of the Netflix drama series Locke and Key, Kinsey Locke (Emilia Jones) goes into her head and takes away her fear. Kinsey, a natural overthinker, believes her fear makes her weak. So she believes the only way to a fearless and satisfied life is to take that emotion away. Things work out for a while. Kinsey is bold, audacious, and vivacious. She puts pink strips in her hair and her whole aura changes. Everyone observes this and loves it for her. And for a while, she basks in the sunny liberation that comes with not being afraid of every little thing. However, existing without fear makes Kinsey impulsive, rude, and careless. She uses her family's magical keys in public and doesn't care that they might be discovered. She is rude to the people that care about her, gets into trouble multiple times, and despite the red flags, gets into a relationship with a malicious entity masquerading as a teenager. Kinsey later realizes that her fear serves a purpose. That it is ok to feel fear now and then. That we should strive to manage fear, not eliminate it. So she sets things right by finding her fear and putting it back into her head.

Emotions are neither bad nor good. They are neutral units of existence that serve a specific. Like Kinsey's fear, your anxiety serves a purpose. It prevents you from staying out late on a Sunday night because you have work the next day. However, when it becomes consistent and unmanageable, it becomes a problem. Consistent anxiety is a feedback loop. It generates nervous unhelpful thoughts that cloud your judgment and creates more anxiety. Studies by Nolen-Hoeksema show that ruminators have more anxiety than the average person. In other words, anxiety and rumination feed off each other, heavily impacting your mood and motivation. So if your thoughts are always making you anxious, you may be an overthinker.

shows that thinking too much.

Avoidance of Previously Pleasurable Activities

In a Tedx Talk titled Writer's Block: A Myth or Not?, poet, essayist, and novelist, Dr. Santosh Bakya charts her experience with writing. As a child, she loved writing, and it came easily to her. Every time she set pen to paper, words flowed in torrents. However, as she grew and met others in the writing field, the pressure to be perfect and produce work that stood out increased. So sometimes, when she set pen to paper, nothing came out. Bakya debunks the myth of writer's block. She believes it is a result of overthinking. In her words, "If plumbers cannot have plumber's block, engineers cannot have engineer's block, and doctors cannot have doctor's block, why then should writers have writer's block?"

While what we perceive to be writer's block can result from improper plotting, world-building, and scene conceptualization, overthinking is usually the prime suspect. When you are overthinking, your thoughts take over your life and make your favorite activities lose their spark. A 1993 study by Lyubomirsky and Nolen-Hoeksema found that, as with depression, people avoid their hobbies when they are overthinking. Their passion for the activity begins to dwindle because of the crippling doubt and anxiety that comes with overthinking. They overthink each word before they write it, and when they finally pen it down, they doubt its rightness.

Reinterpretation of Old Memories

Have you ever found yourself thinking of all the things you should have said in an argument two hours after the argument has ended? Or maybe remembering something embarrassing you did in the 10th grade and cringing at it?

Well, you are not alone. We have all been there.

It is normal to have brief flashbacks about past events. However, the average person lets go of them after a while. The overthinker, on the other hand, settles there. A 2006 study by Starr and Moulds found that ruminators struggling with anxiety and depression replay past events in their heads and try to find new dimensions to them. They blame themselves for all the bad incidences and missed opportunities and chalk up the positive ones to luck. If you find yourself constantly revisiting embarrassing moments and missed opportunities and blaming yourself for them, you are probably an overthinker.

Always Reading Between the Lines

There is a clear line between being perceptive and being an overthinker. The perceptive person notices things the average person takes for granted. They notice that person in the corner that is finding it difficult to interact and socialize. They are an expert of sorts at body language and observe the swift and barely observable change in a person's countenance when a topic is brought up. The overthinker is the same way. However, they make everything about them (e.g. believe the other person is not untercating because they don't like them (the ovethinker).

Whereas the perceptive person's insight comes from a place of great social skills, the overthinker's observations are motivated by a unique type of hypervigilance. More than revisiting a past event, they agonize over the finer details and try to read between the lines—even when there is nothing to be read.

Their eyes looked flat when they smiled at me. Maybe they're pretending and don't actually like me.

Why did she walk away immediately I approached them? Had they been discussing me?

As they always see smoke, even where there is no fire or kindling, they need to be constantly reassured that all is well. So they triangulate and run the situations by multiple friends on different occasions.

Difficulty Sleeping

Imagine you have a drummer for a housemate. They practice all day long, however, the intensity of their practice increases just before bedtime. Chances are you would find it hard to fall asleep with all that infernal drumming. The only difference here is your brain is the drummer housemate. If your brain is always wired and chattering away like magpies in the summer, it will be difficult for you to fall asleep or get quality sleep. Slumber is preceded by a host of unique physiological and biochemical processes. Your heart and breathing rate drop. The muscles relax. Cortisol lowers and the levels of melatonin, the sleep enzyme, increase. All these changes are the markers of relaxation and are the direct opposite of what happens when we are stressed and overthinking. When we are overthinking, the body can go into the stress response (flight or fight mode). Cortisol levels skyrocket as you worry about making it on time to work tomorrow, making it impossible to fall asleep and relax. Your HPA axis (hypothalamus, pituitary, adrenals) is stimulated, and the brain triggers a cascade of neurotransmitters and hormones in the body, which then have physical effects. The muscles tighten, your tongue clings to the roof of your mouth, and your shoulder tense. Your breathing and heart rate quicken, thus destroying the calm necessary for slumber.

Multiple research has shown a comorbidity between rumination/overthinking and poor sleep quality. A 2018 study published in the Journal of Sleep Research, shows that people who succumb to overthinking and rumination are more likely to develop insomnia and other sleep-related disorders. This is in line with a 2002 study stating that overthinkers and people who experienced high levels of pre-bedtime cognitive arousal had more difficulty falling and remaining asleep, experienced generally fragmented sleep, and were more likely to have nightmares.

Physical Fatigue

I had a bad habit of not turning off my laptop. Whenever I want to stop working, I either hibernate it or put it on sleep. I never really shut down my tabs or turned off the computer itself. I carried on like this for months. I noticed a few concerns along the way.

Lags.

Screen freezing.

Longer loading time.

I didn't really take it so serious, neither did I link it to never turning off my system. Till one day, I put it on sleep, and it never came on again. The overthinking brain is like a laptop that is never shut down. Thoughts are never really just thoughts. They can be physically and emotionally draining. The brain makes up a miserly 2% of our body weight. However, it is metabolically expensive as it burns 20% of daily accumulated energy.

Overthinking takes our time, energy, and attention. While the human body is insanely resilient, it was only designed to endure brief and well-spaced moments of acute stress. It buckles under the weight of chronic/ongoing stress. When we overthink, the thalamus also perceives it. The problem is that it cannot separate your negative thoughts (e.g., thinking you look hideous or worrying your partner will leave you) from real danger. So it increases your BP and affects your mood. Exposure to prolonged periods of stress, as seen with consistent overthinking, can also lead to various cardiovascular diseases, hormonal disregulation, muscle tension, migraines, reduced libido, irritability, nervousness, lowered appetite, apathy, and general feelings of fatigue

Development of Other Mental Illnesses

"When there is no enemy within, the enemy outside can do us no harm . . ." is an African proverb that illustrates how an overthinking mind can predispose us to a variety of mental illnesses. Overthinking puts our minds into cognitive overdrive. Constantly analyzing life, self, and actions can leave us feeling stuck, distressed, helpless, and depressed. Thus, it is unsurprising that a strong link exists between rumination (specifically rumination about past events) and mental illnesses like depression, PTSD, and OCD. With healthy self-reflection, the brain sees things more clearly and considers solutions to problems. However, rumination does the opposite; it brings up obstacles for every solution we present. The link between overthinking and other mental illnesses like depression, PTSD, and OCD is a chicken-and-the-egg situation, as both seem to complement each other equally. For example, when a person with depression overthinks and feels bad about their role in the dissolution of a friendship, we know that two forces are in play: rumination/overthinking and depression. However, one cannot say which precedes the other or exerts more influence.

Decreased Problem-Solving Ability

Anxiety affects all aspects of our physical, psychological, social, and spiritual lives. Two things happen to the brain when it overthinks and mostly produces pessimistic thoughts. The first is a general slowing down of the brain and a reduction in cerebellum activity. The latter especially results in difficulty in problem-solving.

The second change takes place in your frontal lobe. The frontal lobe is the site of thought generation and the seat of executive function. It oversees planning, decision-making, problem-solving, impulse inhibition, working memory retention, and other critical cognitive processes. More than these, the frontal lobe is the site of integrating, interpreting, and creating new thoughts and ideas. It decides what is essential and "true" based on what you pay attention to. Thus, the more negative thoughts you chew on, the more neurons it creates to support your negativity.

Consistency and frequency are the common threads linking these markers of overthinking. Losing sleep once in a while about an important event doesn't mean you are an overthinker. Losing motivation for previously enjoyable activities may point to other mental health disorders like depression, not anxiety, and rumination. Feeling fatigued alone doesn't mean you are anxious. It can point to other stressors in your life and immediate environment. For it to be classed as anxiety or overthinking:

- It has to happen repeatedly over a long and observable period.

- You should experience meta-thought and a combination of at least three other factors.

Summary

- Overthinking now and then doesn't make you an overthinker. There are certain key markers of an overthinker and to be labeled as one, you have to exhibit these markers, frequently and consistently.

- The first marker is meta thought, a situation where you are not only thinking about things but also thinking about your thoughts.

- The second is a persistent and consistent inability to make a choice in the face of two or multiple options. This is usually motivated by a fear of making mistakes.

- Next is lack of concentration. Overthinking is like juggling multiple activities at once but never really giving any one of them the attention they deserve. It forces you to think without acting, to move without making progress. You might be an overthinker if you find it hard to concentrate on things because of your riotous thoughts.

- Another is the avoidance of previously enjoyable activities. This is often the reason behind things like creative or writer's block. It is difficult to enjoy your hobbies or pastimes when you constantly overthink and doubt every action you take, design you make, or word you write.

- If you find yourself consistently revisiting past events, arguments, and missed opportunities and blaming yourself for it, then you might be an overthinker.

- The perceptive person notices things the average person misses because of their above-average people skills and desire to be there for others. The overthinker observes things others miss because of their uncharacteristic hypervigilance and desire not to offend anyone. While the perceptive person can observe inconsistencies in body language and speech patterns without personalizing them, the overthinker believes that every negative tic made by the other person is somehow because of them or some fault of theirs.

- If your brain is always wired and chattering away like magpies in the summer, it will be difficult to fall asleep or get quality sleep. Multiple studies have shown a link between overthinking/rumination and the development of insomnia and other sleep disorders.

- The brain makes up a miserly 2% of our body weight. However, it is metabolically expensive as it burns 20% of daily accumulated energy. Overthinking takes our time, energy and can lead to the development of certain cardiovascular diseases.

- Overthinking puts our minds into cognitive overdrive. Thus, it is unsurprising that a strong link exists between rumination (specifically rumination about past events) and depression.

5

Different Strokes, Different Folks: The Different Types of Overthinking

"Worry is the interest paid in advance for a debt you may never owe"

Mark Twain

Overthinking is like an ice-cream shop. It has different flavors, and sometimes, our own version of it might be a combination of two or more types. To know the type—or types—of overthinking you have is to understand the "why" behind it. Do you agonize over the ashes of a toxic relationship, blaming yourself for ever believing their lies in the first place? Do you worry about not making the cut for your preferred school just because you decided to take the weekend off studying? Or maybe you are the type that only worries when picking between two or more choices. Or someone that only overthinks when they are in public settings.

In this chapter, we will examine the different types of overthinking and the thought process that necessitates them.

1. Depressive Rumination

A relationship that was abusive or ended without closure.

A friend that betrayed our trust.

A business partnership that turned out to be a scam. A wrong decision we still cannot forgive ourselves for. We have all been there. Depressive rumination is just like it sounds. Regrets and "Had I known" power this flavor of overthinking. It reminds me of a quote attributed to Lao Tzu:

"If you are depressed, you are living in the Past. If you are anxious, living in the future. If you are at peace, you are living in the moment."

With depressive rumination, we frequently travel to the past, obsess over what happened there and beat up our past selves for not knowing or being better. We cringe at the situationships we entered and use words like "idiot" and "failure" to describe ourselves. Like all things, this kind of rumination has positive and negative aspects. The upside is that you learn from your mistakes and (most times) never repeat them. However, the negatives outweigh the positives. Depressive rumination leads to a negative valuation of self. It also keeps us stuck in the past. Many people believe that always thinking and rehashing past negative experiences prevents them from making the same mistakes. While this can sometimes be true, depressive rumination sometimes keeps us from taking healthy risks and exploring life. We become like the proverbial Chicken Little, expecting the sky to fall each time we encounter a situation remotely similar to the one that did us in.

To rephrase a popular Christian quote, "The idle mind is the workshop of depressive rumination." Unlike other flavors of overthinking, which usually have a clear antecedent, most times, depressive rumination occurs when we have nothing occupying our attention. You can think of it as the overthinking mind's way of keeping itself active and burning calories.

2. Anxious Rumination

This type of rumination is also known as worry about the future. You are lying in bed, and all you can think about is tomorrow.

Will I wake up in time? I didn't wake up in time two days ago. What if it happens today?

Shit, I have a proposal due in a week and haven't even started?

What if I made the wrong choice? I should have picked ecru instead of duck-egg blue.

Unlike the depressive ruminator who travels to the past, the anxious ruminator lives in the future. The depressive ruminator analyzes past situations and blames themselves for it. The anxious ruminator, however, takes it a step further. They analyze past situations, blame themselves for them, and imagine possible future catastrophes based on past software. This version of overthinking is the vanilla flavor of overthinking. It is what comes to everyone's mind when you tell them you are worried or anxious. However, that doesn't make it any less deadly or serious than the rest.

3. Indecisive Rumination

Have you ever spent moments in a mall aisle agonizing over which type of peanut butter to buy? You want to take the smooth one because it glides easier on toast. However, you still hold on to the crunchy one because you like the texture it gives your smoothies. You cannot buy both because your budget only accommodates one. So, you stand there for more minutes than necessary, worrying over which option is right.

Congratulations, you may have indecisive rumination. Also known as analysis paralysis and decision fatigue, indecision rumination is the inability to make decisions in the face of two or more choices. Here, the brain analyzes the available options and turns them over repeatedly without making a choice. While analysis is crucial to the decision-making process, the cycle is incomplete if it does not culminate in a definite choice. People like this are often afraid of making the wrong choices, so they take no action at all. However, they do not realize that inaction is still a decision.

4. Social Anxiety

Picture this. You are at a party. You did not want to go, but your friends insisted. The party was supposed to be so much fun. Grudgingly, you decide to go. Immediately you walk through the doors, you regret that decision. Your heart slams against your chest as multiple pairs of eyes turn to look at you and your friends. Outwardly, you seem calm, but your brain is going haywire.

Crap! I think I just smudged my mascara.

Dear God! We have to go down the stairs. I think I'm going to trip

I shouldn't have come. I'm so awkward, and it's so obvious.

My hands are so sweaty. I'm not going to shake anyone. But what if they take it the wrong way?

This disturbing and judgemental commentary is seemingly out of your control and narrates every little movement you make. It only quietens when you leave the event and are safely ensconced in your own home.

This is social anxiety at its finest. As the name implies, social anxiety is an intense unease in the face of social interaction. While all of us are conscious of committing gaffes in social settings and recover quite quickly when we do, for the socially anxious person, the thought of making a mistake paralyzes them. This makes them come off as more awkward.

The socially anxious brain believes that to be loved and accepted, they must always be—or rather, seem—perfect. They cannot have a hair out of place or laugh too loudly or too long at a joke. This fear usually stems from a history of low self-esteem, abuse, bullying, teasing, or controlling parenting, and it presides over all their social interaction.

5. Catastrophizing

The story below illustrates the unique thought process of the catastrophizing mind:

A man was driving along a dark country road one night when he heard a loud bang! The car jerked to a halt, and the man got out. As the cold wind gusted and numbed his skin, he noticed, with dismay, that he had a flat tire. Ever the problem solver, the man decided to fix the flat himself. Ignoring the sounds of the dark coming from the world around him, he went to his trunk and began pulling out the necessary tools:

A spare tire.

Lug wrench.

With a sinking feeling, the man realized the jack was missing! There was no way he could fix the flat now. He whipped out his phone to call AAA, but there was no reception. The air was getting colder, and the sounds more menacing.

Paralyzed with fear and the cold air, the man was totally at a loss on how to proceed when he saw it, the distant wink of a porch light. Then and there, he makes up his mind to walk over to the house and ask the owner for a jack.

Fueled by the belief that help was on the way, the man made off in the direction of the light. The walk from the car to the house was long and filled with more sounds. As the man put one foot in front of the other, his confidence waned. What was he doing? What were the odds that the house owner would help him or even open the door? The man was probably already in bed and would be mighty pissed at being disturbed. People in this area weren't known to be particularly friendly. What if the house owner set the dog—one of these bloodthirsty pit bulls that have been crossed with different wild animals—on him? Heck, what if he met him at the door with a gun?

This thought stopped the man in his tracks. A shiver racked his frame. He was too far away from his car to go back. However, he was not close enough to the house yet. He could still return to the car, shut himself in, and wait till morning. A howl changed his mind, and he continued walking to the house, but the thoughts kept coming. The house might seem like the safest option, but what if the house owner robs him? At this point, the man feels different emotions: unease, indecision, fear, and anger. But even if the homeowner was a jerk, he really needed that jerk's jack! So he walks up the porch steps, taking them two at a time, and gently raps on the door. Upstairs, a light comes on. There is a shuffle and the quick rat-a-tat of slippers-covered feet coming down the stairs. As the man waits outside, all the emotions reach a crescendo. He is standing, feet shoulder-width apart, tongue ready to explain his reason for being here, fists ready to attack in case the man was hostile.

The door is thrown open, and a groggy-looking man asks, "Can I help you?"

The stranded man shouts, "I don't need your bloody jack, anyway!" and stalks off.

Catastrophizing is (always) imagining the worst-case scenario and acting based on your assumptions. It is waking up in the middle of the night, seeing a figure huddled in a corner, and instead of turning on the light to see it's your coat, you assume it is probably an assassin sent by your ex. Sometimes, catastrophizing doesn't manifest on grand scales like a gun-totting-pitbull-loving homeowner or an assassin. Sometimes, it can be something mild—but still serious—like believing you will probably end up stocking shelves for life because you got a C+ in Math.

6. Neutralizing the Brain Freeze

How do you neutralize the brain freeze that comes with these different flavors of over-thinking?

The Depressive Ruminator has to learn to forgive themselves. You may have ignored everyone and walked into that situation, but everyone makes mistakes. However, our mistakes are not the sum of who we are. This is especially important if your depressive rumination is rooted in abuse. You are the victim. It doesn't matter if the blame stems from others or self, victim-blaming is always in poor taste. Forgive yourself for not seeing the red flags, and move on. The second part of healing is to root yourself in the present. The depressive ruminator has so much mental real estate in the past. There is nothing you can do about the past. Rehashing it and replaying multiple alternative realities won't change what happened. It will not un-break your heart or undo what was done to you. You only have control over the present and what you do in the moment. In a latter chapter, we will look at how you can tether yourself firmly to the present using psychological tools like grounding.

The Anxious Ruminator also needs to learn to live in the present. Like the past, you have no control over the future. The future is dictated by multiple factors over which you have little control. Worry less and do more when you can. Instead of worrying about making the deadline, get started now and do as much as possible. Better to turn it in 80% completed than to turn in nothing. As an anxious ruminator, it can sometimes feel like you are all mind and less body. Thus, stepping out of your head and into your body through grounding exercises becomes especially important.

For the Indecisive Ruminator, the first step to healing is limiting your options. As safe and as logical as it may seem to consider multiple options before making a choice, with you, the more options you have, the harder it is for you to make decisions. You do not need to check out all the brands of peanut butter before making a decision. It is not life and death; it's just spread. The second step is to delineate what matters most to you. This will make deciding easier. For example, when buying groceries, is affordability more important than brand names? When picking a movie, are you more interested in the cast or the storyline? Having these value systems hastens the decision-making process for you. So whenever you are caught between two choices, you refer to your value systems and choose based on them. The second step is to learn to be comfortable with making mistakes. This type of ruminator finds it hard to decide because they fear the consequences of choosing a particular option. It doesn't matter so much when choosing between two peanut butter brands. However, the fear becomes understandable when it comes to more serious affairs like deciding between two jobs, universities, potential partners, etc. However, indecision is still a choice. By not making a decision, you are indirectly rejecting both options—and that is usually not your intention. To err, it is said, is human. We all make mistakes, and sometimes, those mistakes actually orient us on the right path. Do your due diligence, make a choice, realize that you will be fine, and can start over if you made a "wrong choice."

Like the first two groups of overthinkers, the socially anxious person needs to get out of their head. However, it doesn't stop there. (S)he needs to build a strong, positive internal narrative to counter the constant chatter from their overthinking and socially anxious brain. So each time their brain panics about or condemns their actions in social settings, this positive voice checks it. For example, if your brain berates you for smudging your mascara while nervously rubbing your eyes, reply with the following.

"It is not the end of the world. It is just mascara. I'll just go to the powder room and touch up my face."

If your social anxiety stems from your history with controlling parents, re-parent yourself. Your parents may not necessarily be bad people. They probably did the best they could with the tools they had. However, a critical part of adulthood is accepting that your upbringing wasn't the best and becoming the best version of yourself by healing those childhood wounds. Teach your inner child that the perfection your parents demanded is impossible, that it is ok and healthy to make mistakes every now and then, and that it is the so-called imperfections that give life its beautiful texture.

Another way to reduce your anxiety in the face of social interactions is to put yourself out more. Think of it as exposure therapy. Once every week, put yourself out there. Start from as low as 10-20 minutes and work your way up to 4-5 hours. If there is anything humans are good at, it is adaptation. Practice really does make perfect. You will be filled with anxious fear the first few times you try this. You may blunder, be awkward or not interact much with others. However, with subsequent interactions, your brain learns to relax. It knows it's been here before, has made a few errors, and still somehow survived the interactions. A final tip for the socially anxious person is to turn the conversation on the other person. Social anxiety is very self-focused. With it, it is all about "Me, Myself and I"

I am always making mistakes.
What is wrong with me?
I definitely come off as awkward.

With such mental commentary running in your head, relaxing and enjoying the other person's company is impossible. To get around this, center the other person in the conversation. Ask them about themselves, listen to their replies, and ask follow-up questions. If there is anything people like doing, it is talking about themselves. By letting them take center stage in the discussion, you become more relaxed amd make the other person feel seen, heard, and less likely to notice your awkwardness.

Summary

- There are five major flavors of overthinking: depressive rumination, anxious rumination, indecisive rumination, social anxiety, and catastrophizing.

- It is possible to experience a combination of these types of overthinking.

- Depressive Rumination is powered by regrets and "had I knowns" and occurs when we cannot seem to move past a certain event or mistake we made in the past.

- Anxious rumination (textbook anxiety) is also known as worry about the future. The anxious ruminator lives in the future. They analyze past situations, blame themselves for them, and imagine possible future catastrophes based on past software.

- Also known as analysis paralysis and decision fatigue, indecision rumination is the inability to make decisions in the face of two or more choices.

- Social anxiety is an intense unease in the face of social interaction. Here, the individual blows the tiniest mistakes out of proportion and may come off as awkward or shy in social settings.

- Catastrophizing is (always) imagining the worst-case scenario (a catastrophe) and acting based on your assumptions.

- The Depressive Ruminator has to learn to forgive themselves and return to the present.

- The Anxious Ruminator must also learn to live in the present and act instead of worrying.

- The Indecisive Ruminator needs to limit choices, develop a fixed value system that hastens their decision-making process, and believe in their ability to bounce back if their choice turns out to be a mistake.

- The socially anxious person needs to get out of their head, create a positive counter-narrative, reparent themselves (if their social anxiety stems from controlling parents), practice socializing, and center the other person in social interactions.

6

The Cat
in Catastrophizing:
Understanding and
Calming the
Catastrophizing Mind

"Most misunderstandings in the world could be avoided if people would simply take the time to ask,
"What else could this mean?"

Shannon L. Alder

✿

If overthinking was an action movie, catastrophizing will probably be the baddie you face at the end. It is the only type of overthinking that can encompass all the other types of rumination. Let's say someone was ruminating on how they were abused (depressive rumination), they might start believing that they are irrevocably damaged because of the abuse and thus, don't deserve a happily ever after (catastrophizing). As previously stated, catastrophizing is a common cognitive distortion or thinking error where we perceive a situation to be horrible, terrible, and irremediable. A key example would be a mother in a traditional and patriarchal household saying to her daughter, "If you don't do your chores, you will grow into a lazy woman and no one will want to marry you . . ." or someone believing they will not get a job and end up dying homeless on the streets just because they failed trigonometry. Essentially, the catastrophizing person makes a figurative mountain out of a molehill. This thought pattern invites even more anxiety, stresses the brain, leaves us in perpetual fear of failure, causes panic attacks, and **contributes to general and social anxiety.**

However, despite all these, catastrophizing serves some dysfunctional functions:

Functions of Catastrophizing

A Shield Against Disappointment and Uncertainty

Never expect anything from anyone if you want to live a happy life.

Blessed is he who expects nothing, for he shall never be disappointed

The wise expect nothing, and hope for nothing, thus avoiding all disappointment and anxiety.

The secret to happiness is low expectations.

There are multiple variations to this sentiment. Even the renowned Shakespeare is known to have said, "I always feel happy. You know why? Because I don't expect anything from anyone. Expectations always hurt." The common thread between all the expressed ideas is the fear of disappointments and unmet expectations. People generally hope for the best and expect the worst. However, the catastrophizing mind just expects the worst, with no hopes for the best in the horizon.

This kind of dark thinking is an armor of sorts. You cannot disappoint someone who is already disappointed in themselves neither can you reject someone who has already rejected themselves. Rejection is only painful when preceded by hope. Like that person that does something silly and laughs before others do, the catastrophizing mind doesn't feel so bad when bad things happen because they have already thought about and mentally experienced it.

A Source of Motivation

Sometimes, nothing pushes us into action better than some good ol' catatrophizing. You are thinking about staying in and ordering pizza for the third time this week and then the thought comes:

"If I continue like this, I'll end up becoming obese and dying of heart disease." Suddenly, you're up! You turn off your UberEats app, remind yourself you have a chicken casserole in the fridge, and head off to the gym. I'll admit, this kind of thinking is effective in the short term. However, in the long term, it makes us angry, anxious and depressed, overwhelmed, and less functional. Although at first, they both can sound alike, there is a world of difference between a pep-talk and a fear talk. A pep talk aims to correct and encourage. Fear talk, on the other hand, corrects by inspiring fear which can lead to burnout and a sense of helplessness.

The Catastrophizing Bypass

Now that we know what catastrophizing looks like and the functions it serves, the question remains: how do we get around it?

One of the most effective solutions to catastrophizing I have seen was observed between a mutual friend and her son's emotional support animal. Let's call my friend, Dahlia. Dahlia's son had a kitten as an emotional support animal. Dahlia had initially wanted to get him a low-maintenance pet like a guinea pig or a goldfish. But the little boy had taken one look at the wide-eyed feline and had fallen in love. Although Dahlia was petrified of cats, her son's happiness was primary. So they went home with the little bundle of paw-fection.

However, this was just the beginning of the end. Adjusting to the kitty was going to prove to be a challenge. Dahlia was so scared of the cat she couldn't stay in the same room with it. Her husband had to help their son with caring for it as Dahlia always ran when she saw the cat. There was really no known basis for Dahlia's phobia of cats. She had never lived with one, neither had she had a negative encounter with them. The few times she tried touching the cat, she broke out in cold sweat. Although she knew the cat was healthy, vaccinated, and tick-free, in a textbook case of catastrophizing, she worried it'll scratch her and give her Cat Scratch Disease (CSD). She wasn't relaxed in her home anymore, and her stress levels were off the roof. Her boy loved the cat, but he was also unhappy with the upheaval its presence had brought.

One day, her son came into her room and announced, "I think we should take the kitten back to the shelter."

Dahlia was aghast. "Why? I thought you liked her?"

The child shrugged. "I do but I love you too and I want you to be comfortable. You haven't been yourself since she came here."

At this point, Dahlia knew she had to do something about her fear. She decided to test out and work according to her catastrophizing thoughts. She was always so afraid of getting CSD, so she worked with that assumption. Before trying to pet or feed the cat, she would ensure every bit of her body was covered. This gave her some level of mental comfort and allowed her to approach the feline. With time, it felt ridiculous to wear leather gloves and long sleeves while feeding a housepet during summer in Arizona. So slowly, she stopped wearing them. The boots, however, stayed on. Eventually, she got comfortable with the cat brushing against her feet and meowing for pats and slowly, the boots too went off. It's been two years since that incidence and the little cat sleeps on the same bed as Dahlia.

Catatsrophizing can also be observed in workplace settings. A close friend of mine recently discovered she was being paid less than everybody in her skills quartile. She felt unhappy and cheated. Did they not value her input? Did they see her as "less than"? Was it because she was a woman? On and on, the questions swirled like dust devils. Finally, she decided to ask for a raise.

She knew it would not be an easy ask. She prepared arguments to support her case in case the management turned down her request. Backing down was not her option. Studies showed that Fridays were the best day to ask for a raise as everyone was consciously and subconsciously excited about the weekend. So that Friday after her lunchbreak, she walked into her boss's office, bursting with facts and data on her contribution to the company, unwilling to be backed up against a wall. Immediately she got the words, "I'd like a raise, Sir." out, her boss replied calmly.

"Sure. can't think of anyone more deserving. What figure do you have in mind?"

She stood there shocked and confused, with no figure in mind. She had prepared for all (negative) scenarios except the one she wanted.

The first step to dealing with catastrophizing is to confront the catastrophe. With the catastrophizing mind, rejection is a consistent fact of life (which is not untrue). However, the flip side of the uncertainty coin brings "yes-es" and "acceptance" every now and then. If you don't believe a certain company will hire you, apply anyway and prepare for both an acceptance and a rejection. The latter will calm your catastrophizing mind, while the application and the preparation for a positive response will ensure you have the best possible shot at the job.

The Trick of Five

Catstrophizing is like being stuck in a storm. You are stuck in a bad situation and cannot see beyond your present predicament. This is where the trick of five comes in. The trick of five is like a light piercing through the darkness of the storm. It is a mantra of sorts that helps you envisage a life and reality beyond your current situation. Let's say something bad happened (spilling wine on someone at a party, a poor presentation at work, a break up, a failed test), and you find yourself catastrophizing, the trick of five mandates you to stop and ask:

Will it matter five minutes from now?

If the answer is yes, ask yourself if it'll matter five hours from now. If the answer is still yes, consider how important this "failure" will be five days, five weeks, five months, or five years from now. With catastrophizing, the present moment seems endless and consuming. It makes us forget that time washes away all things. Sure, you might remember one or two embarrassing things you did in high school but they do not hold sway in your life anymore. They are, at best, footnotes in the story of your life. This little mantra reminds you of what is important and keeps you from creating monsters out of the shadows in your life.

Accepting Uncertainty

Courage, it is said, is not the absence of fear but the judgment that something else is more important than fear. We catastrophize because we are afraid of and don't know how to deal with uncertainties. Uncertainty is a natural, acceptable part of living a wholehearted life. It is what makes life beautiful. We trick ourselves into believing that if we think about the worst we can prevent it from happening. Usually, it is the opposite. Our negative expectations become a self-fulfilling prophecy. When you think about rejection, you get rejected because you cut yourself off from opportunities or reject yourself first.

Remember the man with the flat tire from the previous chapter? Imagine how differently things would've turned out if he had approached things with this mindset: "Sure, the homeowner may be unfriendly, may ask me to get off his property or not even open the door. But there is a chance that he would be friendly, will give me the jack, and probably even let me use his phone and I am going to take that chance. However, if he does turn out to be mean, I will still be ok."

Positive Motivation

The fear talk that is characteristic of the catastrophizing mind can motivate us into action in the short term. However, positive motivation—correcting and motivating yourself with positive possibilities—is more sustainable. Let your positive goals be your truth north, guiding you towards what you want to achieve. In the weight loss community, male obesity and its effects on esteem are often ignored or skirted around. So it was understandable that my colleague, Jim believed he'd always be the big guy in the group. He was a huge proponent of fear talk. He feared dying of a heart attack or getting a partner only to have them leave him because of his weight. This negative motivation helped him go to the gym five times a week. But halfway into the fourth week, he gassed out. It became an inside joke. "Fourth week Jim" became the workout equivalent of a one-minute man. At one point, Jim gave up on losing weight. Maybe he would always be the big guy and that wasn't a bad thing.

For Jim, the inciting incident for a healthier and consistent workout journey was an AI-generated image. An AI image of what he would look like if he lost weight. That picture became his motivation. It became the display picture for all his social media accounts but more than that, that picture became his true north.

Motivate yourself, not with fear, but by what you want in life and what you hope to achieve. Instead of saying, "I have to go to the gym, so I don't blow up and die of heart disease," say something along the lines of: "I want to go to the gym because I want to get my body into the best possible shape and improve my flexibility. Imagine how awesome it would feel to finally be able to do splits!' Instead of saying "I have to go to school because

I don't want to end up homeless," think, "I have to go to school because I want to be a therapist and help out people."

Summary

- Catastrophizing is a common cognitive distortion or thinking error where we perceive a situation to be horrible, terrible, and irremediable.

- Catasphrophizing serves two dysfunctional functions: it shields us against disappointment and acts as a source of motivation.

- The first step to dealing with catastrophizing is to confront the catastrophe. Prepare yourself for both negative and positive outcomes. The former will calm your catastrophizing mind, while the latter will ensure you have the best possible shot at the job.

- The Trick of Five is effective in calming the catastrophizing mind. Catastrophizing limits our field of vision and convinces us that the current situation is our permanent reality. The Trick of Five shows us this is not true and helps us recalibrate our bearings and remember what is truly important.

- The catastrophizer needs to learn that uncertainty is a natural, acceptable part of living a wholehearted life. Accepting uncertainty is not denying its existence, but rather believing and knowing you'd be fine despite it.

- There is a clear line between a pep talk and a fear talk: one aims to kindly encourage and correct, and the other encourages and corrects by inspiring fear. The fear talk that comes with catastrophizing leads to stress and burnout. In the long term, it is more sustainable to motivate yourself with your dreams and potential positive outcomes.

7

Blurred Lines: The Difference Between Overthinking and Other Healthy Versions of Thought

"Healthy self-reflection is all about learning something about yourself or gaining a new perspective about a situation.

Overthinking involves on dwelling on how badly you feel and thinking about all the things you have no control over."

Amy Morin

Besides being good at coming up with worst case scenarios, overthinkers are skilled in arguing and denying their habit of rumination. They mask this habit as self-reflection/introspection, planning for the future, and self-awareness. Anything but overthinking. It is often said that the first step to healing is admitting you have a problem. In this chapter, I'll help you see the problem clearly by drawing clear distinctions between overthinking and other healthy versions of thought

Overthinking Vs. Self-reflection

As they engage in meta-thought—which is simply thinking about one's thoughts—over-thinkers often think they are practicing self-reflection when they ruminate. But intro-spection is more than just thinking about your thoughts; it is inspecting your thoughts, unraveling them, and trying to find a solution. Think of overthinking as running on a treadmill and introspection as running through a neighborhood. With both of them, you rack up miles. However, when you are on the treadmill, you aren't going anywhere. You are just moving on a single stretch of high-density rubber and that motion can trick us into thinking we are actually covering physical distance.

The gist of overthinking is in the name—it is the act of thinking over, above, and beyond what is necessary without a clear end or solution in mind. Thought and the ability to distill, assess and interrogate our thought process are the primary markers of rationality and the reason for our success as a species. However, if there is no end or solution to your thoughts, it becomes a problem. Thinking for the heck of it—as seen in overthinking—is dangerous and detrimental. It forces us to dwell on the negative feelings brought on by our actions or situations. Self-reflection, on the other hand, is healthy, solution-focused thinking.

Overthinking is punitive. Remember how we said that one reward of overthinking is a false sense of control? Well, when we overthink and beat ourselves up for past mistakes, gaffes, and failures, one thing is certain: we are the ones wearing the boxing gloves. By imagining the worst-case scenarios and running with them, we hurt ourselves and our self-esteem. We question our thoughts—and the actions that arise out of them—to such a point where we lose complete faith in ourselves. Conversely, self-reflection is firm but considerate and empathic. It acknowledges your role in the situation but it doesn't dwell on that. It is forgiving and actively motivates you into looking for ways to remedy the situation.

As an extension of the previous point, overthinking is a one-man dramatic produc-tion where we are both victim and villain and are inexorable on both counts. You self-fla-gellate for not knowing better and for becoming hurt in the process. It is a never-ending process of rebounding between "I should've known better..." and "What is wrong with me." Self-reflection acknowledges you were the victim (or the villain), doesn't fault you for it, and looks for ways to move on and make things better.

Anxiety and Stress: Two Halves of a Worrying Coin

People often use the words "anxiety" and "stress" interchangeably and the fact that they can both give rise to each other doesn't help matters. Psychologist Dr. Sarah Edelman explains that stress is something in the environment, an external pressure placed on us, whereas anxiety is our internal experience of this pressure. So basically anxiety is caused by our unique filtration of different stress/pressures in our external and internal environment.

As we have different internal resources through which we process stress, people do not react the same way to the same stressful event. For example, someone that is naturally self-conscious may feel anxious in the face of the stressful experience of a bad hair day. They might feel that bad things always happen to them and decide they are unattractive because their hair is not cooperating. Conversely, someone that is more self-assured, may laugh it off or pop on a hat and be on their merry way. They would not personalize the experience or use it as a metric for their attractiveness.

When we equate stress to anxiety, it is easy to believe stress is negative. This cannot be further from the truth. Stress is an important part of existence. In fact, one primary characteristic of living things is irritability or reaction to stimuli/stress. So stress can be positive. In 1974, endocrinologist and founder of the stress theory, Hans Selye proposed a two-axis, four-component model of stress:'

Low Impact Stress	High Impact Stress
Eustress	Distress
Hypostress	Hyperstress

Figure 1: Hans Selye's Stress Model

When stress is positive, it converts our natural inertia into dynamic action. This good type of stress is called **eustress**. The Greek root word, "_eu_" translates to "good." Thus, eustress is a positive type of stress that keeps us on our toes and propels us to act on our goals and desires. This type of stress is also called curative stress as it brings fulfillment and contentment. Think about when you are lost in the flow when you are doing an activity you love. That thing surging in your veins, that force that keeps you motivated, focused but content is eustress.

When stress tiptoes into the danger zone, it is called **distress**. The Latin root word "dis" refers to "pulling apart or asunder." Thus, you can think of this type of stress as stress that tears us apart internally and places more pressure on our internal and external resources. Distress can further be divided into **acute stress** (brief periods of pressure e.g. while preparing for an exam) and **chronic stress** (e.g. pressure experienced by constantly sampling negative thoughts.)

There is a third type of stress called **hyperstress**. As the prefix "hyper" suggests, this type of stress is caused by overexertion of our physical, mental, or emotional resources and can be observed when we overwork ourselves. Like distress, hyperstress is a high-impact and negative type of stress. With it, we become walking firecrackers, supercharged and ready to go off at the slightest provocation.

The last type of stress is **hypostress**. It is a low-impact type of stress that is brought about boredom and a lack of inspiration. Hypostress is experienced by people who have outgrown their current job/job description, people who work repetitive/monotonous jobs that give little or no mental stimulation e.g. working on an assembly line or as a parcel sorter. Hypostress is characterized by restlessness and boredom.

What we call "stress" in everyday parlance is usually some form or mix of hyperstress and distress. This is usually what kicks off our body's fight or flight response, exhausts and overwhelms us, and causes burnout. To flourish, we do not need a "stress-free" life. What we need is a balance between all the types of stress. Selye recommends "fighting for the highest possible aim (by increasing eustress as much as possible and mobilizing the minimum required level of hyperstress and distress) but never putting up resistance in vain (knowing when to fall back into hypostress).

Rumination vs Self Awareness

Rumination is the recycling of thoughts and persistent worry and brooding. Thoughts are unpredictable and not necessarily true. Depending on the state of mind you find yourself in, your thoughts can sometimes "present evidence" to support an idea it has. For example, a friend asks you for a loan. You decline because you're in a financial fix. However, you find yourself unable to let go of the situation. Your friend and late replies go together like maple syrup and pancakes. However, since that incident, anytime they take time to reply to your texts, you can't help wondering if it's because of the loan. Your start to think: "Maybe I'm not a good friend. Maybe I should have given him half. My salary comes in a week. I could manage till then..."

Self-awareness is a different game altogether. It is knowledge of the cumulative of our thoughts, feelings, character, and action. With it, our impression of self doesn't change in the face of new situations. We know who we are and even when we do things that may cause some awkwardness, that knowledge of self doesn't fade. A self-aware person understands that saying no to a loan when they're in a financial fix makes them a wise person, not a bad friend.

Overthinking is like scanning a book, homing in on a single line, and judging the entire book based on that line. However, self-awareness is knowing that book completely because you have read it from cover to cover multiple times and understanding that the book is a sum of its parts, not defined by some of its parts. Awareness is not judgment. It is simply checking in and taking stock of our internal resources (thoughts, character, feelings) and external resources (bodily sensations) and using the information as a guide in our daily interactions with the rest of the world.

A Bit of Housecleaning

The most important rule of screenwriting is that characters are defined, not by what they say or think, but by what they do. Based on this, my friend, it is important to remember that you are not your thoughts. Thoughts are elusive things. They only become important when they are translated into action. If they remain in the abstract realm, then you still have power over them. Many overthinkers judge themselves harshly because of their thoughts. You're not in a good mood and your partner isn't helping matters by nagging. The thought comes in: "I wish they'd just leave me alone." All of a sudden, you feel bad.

Why did I think that?

I must be a terrible person. They only want the best for me.

And just like that, a bad day becomes even worse. While our thoughts can control most aspects of our lives, it is important to remember that you are not your thoughts. Your actions are what make you who you are. Just like you cannot "think" your way into medical school (i.e. you have to do the work to become a doctor), having the odd, intrusive, negative thought doesn't make you a bad person.

Think of your thoughts as fishes in a river. You are watching them float by. They come and go as they please. However, a thought (or a fish, as per the analogy) only becomes important when you reach out and grab it. This is the theory of **cognitive fusion.** The brain is a word machine that chatters on and on and on. With cognitive fusion, we buy into every little thought that this chattering machine pumps out. The goal is to practice **cognitive diffusion,** which is a separation of self from your thoughts. To paraphrase a quote from Eckhart Tolle "When we realize that the voice in our head is not who we are and that we are just observers of our thoughts, we become truly liberated." Charting the same course as Tolle, the Indian guru, Sadghuru recommends thinking of overthinking as mental diarrhea. The first step to curing physical diarrhea is to stop eating/consuming. Thus, the first step to curing mental diarrhea is cognitive diffusion, or the refusal to consume every negative thought that crosses your mental lunch table.

Summary

- Besides being good at coming up with worst-case scenarios, overthinkers are skilled in arguing and denying their habit of rumination. They mask this habit as self-reflection/introspection, planning for the future, and self-awareness.

- As they engage in meta-thought—which is simply thinking about one's thoughts—overthinkers often think they are practicing self-reflection when they ruminate.

- The gist of overthinking is in the name—it is the act of thinking over, above, and beyond what is necessary without a clear end or solution in mind. Self-reflection, on the other hand, is healthy, solution-focused thinking.

- Overthinking is punitive. It is a one-man dramatic production where we are both victim and villain and are inexorable on both counts. Conversely, self-reflection is firm but considerate and empathic. It acknowledges your role in the situation but it doesn't dwell on that. It is forgiving and actively motivates you into looking for ways to remedy the situation.

- Though anxiety and stress can give rise to each other, they are not the same thing

- Psychologist Dr. Sarah Edelman explains that stress is something in the environment, an external pressure placed on us, whereas anxiety is our internal experience of this pressure.

- Endocrinologist Hans Selye propounded a two-axis, four-component model of stress. The four types of stress according to Selye are eustress, distress, hyperstress, and hypostress.

- Eustress is a positive type of stress that keeps us on our toes and propels us to act on our goals and desires.

- Distress is a high-impact type of stress that tears us apart internally and places more pressure on our internal and external resources. It can further be divided into acute stress and chronic stress.

- Hyperstress is another type of high-impact stress caused by overexertion of our physical, mental, or emotional resources and can be observed when we overwork ourselves.

- Hypostress is a low-impact type of stress that is brought about by boredom and lack of inspiration.

- Rumination is the recycling of thoughts and persistent worry and brooding. Self-awareness is knowledge of the cumulative of our thoughts, feelings, character, and action. With it, our impression of self doesn't change in the face of new situations. We know who we are and even when we do things that may cause some awkwardness, that knowledge of self doesn't fade.

- Cognitive fusion is where we buy into every little thought that crosses our mind. This is the primary habit of the overthinker. Conversely, cognitive diffusion is the understanding that we are not our thoughts but rather, observers of said thoughts. With this understanding, we do not buy into every thought we think.

8

The Rules of Engagement: 13 Methods to Hacking the Wired Mind

"So many thoughts, my Kvothe. You know too much to be happy. "

Patrick Rothfuss (The Wise Man's Fear)

It is said that we cannot think our way out of a problem using the same thinking that got us into it in the first place. Continuing on that path and expecting different results is akin to madness. If the chapters before have shown us anything, it is that overthinking serves very little purpose, makes us less productive, and can impede our ability to solve problems. The major problem overthinkers have lies in the way they engage with the world within and around them. In this chapter, we will establish new rules that will change your mindset and guide your interpersonal and intrapersonal relationships.

1. Get Comfortable With Making People Uncomfortable

It doesn't matter if you bend yourself into a pretzel, you cannot and will never make everyone happy. There is no need overthinking and benching your needs just to make the other person feel comfortable. Assertiveness can be awkward at first, especially when people are used to you being a yes-man. It can be quite a shock hearing you say no when they are used to you going along with things. Get used to making people uncomfortable, especially in situations where your needs are being overlooked. You cannot control the situation or people's response to it. The only thing you have control over is your own response. Learn to put yourself first and not worry about how people react. Do you and focus on you; the rest of the world will adjust.

2. Learn your Triggers

Like all habits, it can sometimes seem like our rumination is unprompted and unpredictable, but it is not. No two overthinkers are the same. They overthink at different levels, at different times of the day, and for different reasons. Thus, the onus is on you to identify your triggers and the conditions that make you more susceptible to rumination. The **Antecedent Behavior and Consequence (ABC) model** helps us to identify triggers and patterns to the habit of rumination by looking at what precedes (antecedent) and follows (consequence) a behavior or thought process. An **antecedent** is simply something that kicks off a behavior. The **behavior** is the result of the trigger, and the **consequence** is the outcome. For example: when you are watching a movie (antecedent), you always eat snacks (behavior) after the movie is finished, you feet bad because you overate (consequence). Following this x-ray, you realize the problem is not overeating but rather the associations your mind makes between cinema and food. Using this model, try and pinpoint the following:

- What time of day are you most likely to ruminate (Before bed or in the middle of the workday? When something good happens or when you are alone?)

- Where are you most likely to overthink (at home, work, alone, at the bar?)

- What situations trigger it? (e.g., Right after a social situation or argument? After mindlessly scrolling through social media?)

- Your body language when you overthink (Is your jaw tight? Are you grinding your teeth? Are you shaking your legs or jiggling the keys? Is your tongue clinging to the roof of your mouth? Are your hands restless?)

3. Schedule Overthinking

"Delay, don't deny" is a primary rule of healthy dieting. This rule can be extended to overthinking. When dieting, studies have shown that people with restrictive diets (diets that demonize sweets, carbs, and the occasional bag of chips) are more likely to fall off the wagon and binge on food. In the same way, when you bar your brain from overthinking, it does the opposite, and the situation worsens.

The "delay, don't deny" rule enjoins you to postpone eating desserts but not cut them off. One way to do this is by scheduling cheat days or eating your sweets last after eating a regular portion of healthy food. By doing the latter, your stomach doesn't have as much space for sweet consumption. In the same vein, overthinking is a natural phenomenon. The problem is when it becomes too frequent. Based on this, it is impossible to never overthink. So instead of cutting overthinking out of your mental diet, postpone or schedule it. Instead of saying, "I'll not worry about this." say, "I'll worry about this later," or "I'll worry about this at the close of work." When you put it this way, your brain thinks, "It is a date." Also, it is not enough to just schedule overthinking, ensure you honor the date and set a time limit for overthinking. It might seem counterproductive, but using that allotted time to worry about that situation is effective. E.g., "I'll worry about my work conditions for one hour starting at 6 p.m. on Friday." This overthinking schedule gives your overthinking brain the workout it needs and the impression of control.

4. Never Worry in Your Head

In Seneca's words, "We suffer more in our head than in reality." Overthinking forces us to keep things in our head, and like shadows forming scary images across a wall, our thoughts are stronger, scarier, and insurmountable when they are in our headspace.

The solution?

Put them down. Externalize them.

Have you ever started talking to someone about a problem and realized halfway in that you have come upon the solution? Well, writing down your thoughts works in the same way. Writing is a psychomotor skill. It mobilizes your physical and mental resources. As one writes, they indirectly reflex—not ruminate—on the situation, thus gaining insight on how to resolve the problem. Another positive about this is it can also be very helpful in tracking your triggers and certain constant thought patterns you may not have been aware of. So write it down. It doesn't matter how inconsequential or random you feel the thought is. Write it down and gain clarity.

5. Replace the Negative Thoughts

Nature is the great equalizer. With it, every unit has an antithesis, and every negative, a neutralizing positive. As nature abhors a vacuum, to effectively eradicate negative thoughts and thought patterns, replace them with their positive versions. Studies by the Gottman Institute discovered something affectionately called the magic ratio of relationship success. Conflict and negativity are central parts of our intrapersonal and interpersonal relationships. However, these researchers found a special ratio that determined the lasting potential of a relationship. That magic ratio is 5:1. This simply means that although conflict is unavoidable, for every relationship to last, for every negative/conflict-ridden interaction, there should be at least five positive interactions.

I want you to apply the same principle to your thoughts. Offset each negative thought with five positive ones. Let's say you keep ruminating about your abusive relationship that ended two years ago. You blame and call yourself "stupid" for not seeing the siren-loud red flags. And deep down, believe you are damaged because of it. Swap these negative thoughts and self-impression with something like this:

I made a mistake in accepting them. However, I am not the loser here; they are. I am amazing, thoughtful, kind, and intelligent (feel free to add more positives). They are the loser for treating me badly and letting someone as wonderful as I am go. While I may have scars from this relationship, I am not damaged. Some relationships teach you what to avoid and not tolerate. This was one of them.

You can also use this for simpler negative thoughts. E.g., Whenever you think, "I cannot get anything right," just because you made a mistake, remind yourself that though you fumbled in the current situation, your antecedents prove that you do get other things right. Thus, swap "I cannot get anything right" with this thought:

I may have made a mistake now, but I do get things right. I come to work on time (1), I always hit my KPIS (2), I am a thoughtful partner (3), a wonderful mother/father/uncle/aunt/sibling (4), and a talented artist/writer/professional/teacher (5).

6. Practice Gratitude

As previously mentioned, overthinking robs us of the gratitude gene. It makes us see valleys instead of mountains and shadows instead of light. By cultivating an attitude of gratitude, we win one-half of the battle against overthinking. Make a conscious effort to find things to love, like, and appreciate. Write down things you are grateful for and happy about. It could be things as minor as your favorite food, bar, or restaurant or major things like your career, how close your family members are or how beautiful your body is. Immediately you wake up, and before you go to bed, list five things you are grateful for. This sets the tone for a new day and at night, quietens your mind enough for slumber. You can also have a gratitude journal where you write things you are grateful for and the compliments you receive daily. This journal will act as a source of strength when your mind tries to talk you down or make you feel worthless and unloved.

7. Mindfulness

With overthinking and rumination, we become time travelers, either living in the ruins of the past or the vagueness of the future. Thus, it becomes important to tether and pin ourselves to the present. One way to do this is through mindfulness.

Mindfulness is simply being fully immersed in the currents of the present moments and enjoying all the joys it brings. Eckhart Tolle puts it simply by defining it as "focusing all your attention on the now..." When you are in a social setting and find yourself becoming anxious, turn your attention away from the inner world of overthinking to the outside world of the present. Let the music playing wash over you. Observe the other person's mannerisms, how their eyes crinkle when they smile, and how their laughter comes in rolling waves. Feel the breeze on your skin, the different voices melding into one, and the pleasure of being part of this beautiful moment.

8. Grounding

As an overthinker, it can often feel like you are all mind and no body, all thought and no feeling. This is because you are so used to living in your head and in the past and future that your body and the present feel so alien. Thus, it is not uncommon—especially when we are anxious—to go through the motions without actually feeling anything. We eat without tasting the food. We shower and don't exactly register the sweet scent of the shower gels and the pleasure-pain feeling of the hot water hitting our skin.

This is where grounding comes in.

As the name suggests, this is a practice that brings us back to the terra firma of the present. Unlike the mind, which can be everywhere and anywhere all at once, your body can only be in one place: the now. By mobilizing all our five senses, the 5-4-3-2-1 grounding technique returns us back to the now, one step at a time. So how do you practice this technique? You practice it by highlighting:

- **5** things you can **see**

- **4** things you can **feel** or touch

- **3** things you can **hear**

- **2** things you can **perceive** or smell

- **1** thing you can **taste.**

So when next you start overthinking or worrying, take calm breaths and look around you. Find **five** things you can **see**. This can be the calico cat by your feet, the water stain on your ceiling, or the flower prints on your duvet. Next, find **four** things you can **feel** or touch. This could be the froth of hair on your arms, the scratchy carpet underneath your feet, or the glossy surface of the novel you are reading. Then, focus on **three** things you can **hear**, This could be the good-natured hum of the AC, the delicate pants of your dog, the rustle of the breeze, or the zinging of cars outside your window. Next, identify **two** things you can **perceive** or smell. This could be the lingering smell of your ramen dinner, the scent of fabric softener on your clothes, or the earthy smell of coffee on your breath. Finally, focus on **one** thing you can **taste.** This could be the spicy tingles from your lunch, the fizz of the Dr/ Pepper you just drank, etc. By the time this cycle is complete, you feel more settled into your body and less caught up in your head. If you are a true overthinker, chances are you will worry about getting this sequence correctly. Use the sentence below to remember the order:

Slowly **F**ollow **H**oming **P**igeons **T**oday

5   4   3   2   1

9. Identify and Resolve Cognitive Distortions

We all have faulty beliefs and negative thought patterns that facilitate rumination and overthinking. These beliefs and thought patterns are called cognitive distortions. As the name implies, cognitive distortions are twisted or exaggerated thoughts and beliefs we may have about ourselves, our lives, and our environment. These cognitive distortions are largely formed by our upbringing and are filters through which we pass on all our life experiences. Some of the common types of cognitive distortions include.

All-or-nothing thinking

This is a black-and-white pattern of thought that gives no room for nuance or gray areas. With the all-or-nothing thinker, you are either for them or against them, no compromise, no negotiation. With this binary type of thought, one negative is all it takes to cancel out 99 positives. All-or-nothing thinking s is very common with anxiety, depression, eating disorders, and PTSD. Examples include:

- Thinking you have to go 24 hours without eating after bingeing on food.

- Believing no one loves you, because you had an argument with a friend.

- Believing someone hates and wants to harm you because they share different beliefs.

- Thinking "I am a failure" just because you made a minor mistake.

Overgeneralization

This is an extension of binary/all-or-nothing thinking. However, we take things a step forward by painting life and people with broad brushes based on our limited experiences. Basically, overgeneralization is like a magnifying glass that discounts the positive, enlarges minute negative experiences, and uses them to weave a narrative. Some examples include:

- Thinking, "all men/women/members of a specific socioeconomic class are like this," when the truth is it was just one man/woman/member of a specific socioeconomic class that you met that was like that.

- Thinking "Nothing ever works out for me' when the truth is your life has had many high points.

- Believing the thought "Bad things always happen to me" whereas life is a mixed bag with bad and good things happening to everyone.

With this bias, we make the bad the norm and term "the good" a fluke, random exceptions that do not make the rule.

Internalizing or Externalizing

As the name implies, internalizing is a cognitive bias where we blame ourselves for everything that happens around us. E.g., a child believing her father died because she was naughty at school or someone believing they are the reason for their partner's infidelity. Externalization is the reverse. This is where we see ourselves as blameless and peg all our mistakes and wrongdoings on others and the external environment. E.g., saying you failed a test because the teacher doesn't like you and is out to get you.

Emotional Reasoning

Here, our emotions become the foundation of our beliefs. The thought pattern of the emotional reasoner goes like this: "I feel, therefore, it must be." Thus, their emotions become the facts and the premise on which life-changing decisions are made. E.g., believing that someone hates them just because they got a bad vibe from the person.

As this bias can sometimes yield correct answers, it is especially dangerous. Biases like all-or-nothing thinking are easy to avoid as they are always wrong. However, emotional reasoning is a different type of animal. To resolve it, you must realize the end doesn't always justify the means. The means is just as important as the end. Let's use a mathematical analogy to drive this home. Two people have to solve the math problem 2^2. One resolves it by simplifying it thus: 2 X 2. The other chooses a different approach and solves it by saying 2+2. Both will arrive at the same answer: 4. However, the second person got lucky. They used a faulty method to arrive at a correct answer. As faulty methods are inconsistent, unreliable, and irreproducible, the results will not be correct for problems like 3^2, 4^2, or 5^2. Similarly, using emotional reasoning to arrive at a correct prediction doesn't make the method right.

Magical Thinking

This is a cognitive bias where everything is a sign waiting to be read. To the magical thinker, random events are divine signs that should be heeded without fail. Like the person flipping a coin on all major decisions, the magical thinker reads the tea leaves of random events and makes decisions and assumptions based on them. E.g., Believing you will have an accident if you leave the house because you saw a black cat playing with a saltshaker on a crack in the road.

Do any of these look familiar? Are you fond of assuming someone hates you once they criticize you? (all-or-nothing thinking) Or maybe you are a huge proponent that male/female nature is treacherous and women/men are incapable of love (overgeneralization) because someone under that umbrella hurt you? Well, it gets worse. When we overthink, we tend to worsen the situation by daisy-chaining these cognitive biases. We fear our partner has been unfaithful because of a dream we had (magical thinking), and we believe that fear (emotional thinking). We blame this supposed infidelity on our perceived unlovability (internalization). Identify these cognitive biases immediately you start engaging in them and counter them after the other. Let's try it together using the above scenario as an example:

Thought 1: I had a dream that they cheated. They are probably cheating.

Counter thought 1: This is magical thinking and emotional reasoning. They haven't given me a reason to doubt their fidelity. I cannot base my decisions on dreams. Sometimes our subconscious and conscious thoughts manifest in our dreams, but that doesn't mean they are true.

Thought 2: They are cheating because I am unlovable.

Counter thought 2: I am not unlovable. I am an amazing, friendly, wonderful (add as many qualities as you want) person. I am worthy and deserving of the love I give and receive.

10. Move on quickly

Rumination is a bit like worrying a pimple or picking at a scar. You wake up and see a huge zit on your nose. Years of passive and active skincare knowledge tell you not to pick at it, but you cannot help it. You know that picking at it won't make it go away but you still can't stop. Weirdly, you derive a strange sense of satisfaction from picking at this inflamed hump of sebum-filled flesh.

This is exactly how rumination works.

We know thinking about what is passed won't change it. But we keep replaying it, carefully acting out what we should have said. With overthinking comes the unconscious belief that we can control the past (or future) by reaching back (or forward)and prodding at it.

Stop.

Take a deep breath.

Feel the feelings the situation triggers: embarrassment for tripping down the stairs, anger at being abused, fear about the interview, etc. Then let it go, and move on quickly. Notice the pimple, put down the mirror, and forget about it.

11. Take action

Rumination is all motion and no action. We analyze every possible reality and account for every eventuality, but we still stay rooted to the spot, unable to move. We focus so much on thinking about the actions we should and should not take that we neglect to do what is most important: take action. Bypass the overthinking roadblock and learn to take action swiftly. When a project is placed before you, reschedule worrying about your delivery, and get to work. Don't fall into the trap of thinking about what to do. Be like Nike and ust do it.

12. Focus on Things in Your Locus of Control

It is often said that when the student is ready, the teacher appears. For me, my teacher was a kid's book called *The Boy, the Horse, the Fox, and the Mole,* and it goes:
  A boy and a horse are in the woods, and the boy says to the horse, "I can't see a way through."
  "Can you see your next step?" asks the horse.
  The boy nods. "Yes."
  "Good," neighs the horse. "Then just take that."
  This might seem like a silly kid's story, but it teaches an important lesson about control. When we overthink, we tend to focus on things that are outside our loci of control. We look at how long a journey is and feel overwhelmed. We think about how we have two hours of workouts in front of us or the 14-hour workday we have tomorrow. Instead of worrying about that, worry about the now and what is within your control. Don't worry about the next three sets of exercises you have to do. Worry about the rep you are doing. Instead of worrying about your future career trajectory, focus on acquiring skills. Don't worry about getting a partner that will love and appreciate you. Focus on being someone that is loveable and worthy of appreciation. By focusing on your unique loci of control and exploring what you are responsible for, you take back power and are able to approach life more calmly and rationally.

13. The Four-Way Test: Avoid, Alter, Accept, and Adapt

In the face of life's storms and stressors, we can only avoid, alter, accept or adapt. While there are many things outside our control, we still have agency and retain the right to either engage or **avoid** certain circumstances. Some things that stress us and push us to overthink are things that can easily be avoided. You can avoid that extra workload by simply saying "no" when your friend asks you to do their work for them. You can avoid stress by avoiding a party with many annoying mutual friends. Avoiding is not really evading responsibility or burying your head in the sand, hoping that problems go away. It is the understanding that not everything—or everyone—deserves your time and energy and being conscious of where you channel your mental, physical, and temporal resources.

For things we cannot avoid, we **alter** them. Let's say you live in a house share with two people, and they are both fond of blasting rock music right before bedtime. Moving out is not an option as the house is only a five-minute walk from your office, and you still have 11 months left on your lease. Since you cannot avoid, you can alter the situation by asking your housemates to change/alter their behavior or bringing in a higher, external authority (e.g., a landlord) to make them do so. Effective communication is an important part of this step. Use active and "I" statements to communicate and negotiate your needs. Don't call them insensitive and rude. Say something along the lines of: "I have issues sleeping, and those issues are worsened by the loud music you play at night. Please could you just play the music during the day and keep things calm at night?"

For situations we cannot avoid or alter, we must learn to **accept** and live with them. For example, you cannot really avoid or alter a breakup. You must accept it was good while it lasted and that now, things have changed. No amount of begging, self-flagellation, and "what ifs" will bring them back. Acceptance is not really about giving up or being 100% on board with what happened; it is all about understanding that sometimes, all you can do is make peace with a situation and look for happiness elsewhere.

Sometimes, accepting a situation may not be the right or terminal approach, especially when the problem in question is caused by us and our values, belief systems, or habits. For situations like these, we must go a step further and learn to **adapt.** Adaptation is a core part of our nature; it is changing ourselves internally and externally to match the demands of our environment. Let's imagine you are a night owl, who functions better between the hours of 9 p.m. and 3 a.m. You may avoid day shifts like the plague, sometimes go for jobs that give you the opportunity to work a night shift, and accept that a regular 9-5 may not be your thing. However, if or when you have kids, you are going to have to adapt to working and being up during the day.

With adaptation, we become chameleons, remaining fundamentally the same but changing specific aspects of ourselves to match our social ecosystem. For someone whose overthinking stems from people pleasing, this might look like changing your mindset and becoming comfortable with saying no to people—especially the ones you love.

So before you overthink a situation, think to yourself, ask yourself these questions:

Can I avoid it?

Can I alter it?

Can I accept it and move on?

Can I adapt to it?

This four-way test is the heavy artillery in the fight against overthinking and rumination. It brings things—no matter how complex and difficult they may seem—back into your orbit of control.

Summary

- Get comfortable with the fact that your assertiveness will discomfort others

- Use the Antecedent Bahvior Cinsequence (ABC) model to learn your triggers

- Use the "delay, don't deny" framework to postpone and schedule overthinking

- Journal. Never worry in your head.

- Replace each negative thought with five positive ones

- Practice gratitude and be thankful for the little things.

- Mindfulness is the total and complete immersion in the present and enjoying all the joys it brings. Learn to live in the now. There is no greater moment than the present.

- As an overthinker, it can often feel like you are all mind and no body, all thought and no feeling. Thus, it is not uncommon—especially when we are anxious—to go through the motions without feeling anything. Grounding brings us back to the terra firma of the present by reconnecting us with our five senses.

- As humans, we engage in different cognitive distortions. Some of them are: all-or-nothing thinking, overgeneralization, internalization/externalization, magical thinking, emotional reasoning, etc. During bouts of rumination, we can sometimes daisy-chain some of these cognitive distortions. To solve this, catch yourself when you go down the cognitive distortion rabbit hole and counter each distortion with a rational thought/assertion.

- With overthinking comes the unconscious belief that we can control the past (or future) by reaching back (or forward) and prodding at it. Stop. Take a deep breath. Feel the feelings the situation triggers. Then let it go, and move on quickly.

- Rumination is all motion and no action. Bypass the overthinking roadblock and learn to take action swiftly.

- When we overthink, we tend to focus on things that are outside our locus of control. By focusing on your unique locus of control and exploring what you are responsible for, you take back power and are able to approach life more calmly and rationally.

9

Conclusion

The things that matter are often the smallest. The twinkle in your partner's eyes when they say "I love you." Your child's enthusiastic hug when you tuck them into bed. The excitement on your blood as you tackle a project you are passionate about. One thing all these have in common is they all—if you are lucky—exist in the present. Unfortunately when you overthink, you never really stop to smell the roses. In hot pursuit of the shadows of the past and the wraiths of the future, you miss everything worth feeling. Trying to escape the mind can be a bit like trying to outrun your shadow. Your mind illuminates and magnifies your flaws each time, thus trapping you in its dark grips. Gaining mastery of one's mind is a consistent and ongoing process; it never really ends. Settling in the present, identifying and rejecting cognitive distortions and swapping excessive thought for swift action are all handy tools. However, all these pale in comparison to self-compassion and forgiveness. This is a long journey and the battle is against an adversary that knows you the best. The overthinking mind quails and calms in the face of unconditional self-compassion and forgiveness. It knows that no matter the flaws or mistakes it highlights, you will make peace with them, forgive yourself and move on.

So stop, live in the now, smell the roses and forgive yourself when you make mistakes.

Enjoyed *Rewiring the Anxious Brain*? Share Your Thoughts!

Your insights can guide others in their journey towards better mental health.

By leaving a review on Amazon, you not only help fellow readers make informed decisions but also support our community in growing stronger together.

It's quick and simple, yet it makes a big difference.

Leave a Review today and let others benefit from your experience:

https://amzn.to/3ZkIdqS

Thank you for being a valuable part of this community!

Ready to Dive Deeper? Unlock Your Exclusive Bonus Guides

Professional Resources + Ongoing Support, Tailored to Your Growth

Elevate your personal growth with access to **three short, professional online courses**, available in eBooks (PDF, EPUB, MOBI) and **audiobooks (MP3 files)**, plus an **exclusive email series** delivered to your inbox every few days.

Here's what you'll receive:

- **Enhance Your Communication Skills** – Build meaningful relationships and improve your social intelligence.

- **The Self-Discipline Blueprint** – Cultivate lasting focus and mental resilience to achieve your goals.

- **Mindfulness-Based Stress Management** – Practical techniques to reduce anxiety and maintain calm in any situation.

In addition to these guides, you'll receive a **series of 15-30 short, to-the-point emails** on your chosen topic, sent every 5-6 days. These emails are designed to respect your time while providing actionable insights, tips, and strategies to help you seamlessly apply what you learn to your daily life.

Rest assured, **you won't be spammed**. Alongside valuable guidance, you'll also receive **exclusive free and bargain offers** on books and audiobooks from the author, curated to support your journey.

By joining my mailing list, you'll unlock:

- **Free access** to all three guides (eBook and audiobook formats).

- A **personalized email series** to keep you inspired and motivated.

- **Exclusive tips, offers, and updates** on books, audiobooks, and courses designed for your growth.

Claim Your Free Guides and Email Course Now:

https://bit.ly/3freeguides

Think of it as having a **dedicated mentor in your inbox**, guiding you step-by-step toward a better version of yourself—**no fluff, just value.**

For Audiobook Lovers:

Here's an exclusive offer: you can get one of my audiobooks for free when you sign up for an Audible free trial. Audiobooks make learning both enjoyable and convenient by providing flexibility and immersive experiences.

Why Choose Audiobooks?

-**Listen Anytime, Anywhere:** Make the most of your commute, workout, or daily chores while improving your communication skills.

-**Engage with Voice-Driven Learning:** Listening to professional narration brings concepts to life, making it easier to understand and apply.

-**Learn on the Go:** Master essential lessons seamlessly within your routine.

Special Offer for Eligible Countries

If you're in the USA, UK, Canada, Australia, Germany, or France, you can start listening with your free audiobook by signing up here:

https://bit.ly/freemindfulnessbook

While only one of my audiobooks is included in the free trial, you'll also unlock additional Audible benefits, including monthly credits to choose any audiobook and discounts on future purchases

Until Next Time, stay calm, stay balanced, and keep striving for peace.

Warm regards,

Ian Tuhovsky

10

About Ian Tuhovsky

I an has traveled to over 60 countries, gaining a deep understanding of human connection across cultures.

With over a decade in Human Resources consulting for major corporations, he's developed expertise in communication, discipline, and navigating high-stress environments.

Known for his work in helping professionals build resilience and excel in demanding careers, Ian's books offer practical, research-based strategies for career success and personal growth.

Having personally overcome the challenges of high-pressure settings, Ian brings a compassionate, relatable approach to his writing.

His books have earned thousands of positive reviews, praised for their actionable insights and effectiveness in helping readers achieve discipline, focus, and career fulfillment.

Join the community of professionals who've transformed their lives with Ian's proven guidance for meaningful connections and success in any environment.

Quickly discover author's full book catalogue by just scanning the QR code with your phone:

Printed in Dunstable, United Kingdom

64447654R00057